2013

Bangalore

Author. Jay Kay
Author of The Incredible
Messiah

*India lives in her seven
hundred thousand villages...*
- Mahatma Gandhi

A SILENT

REVOLUTION

*(This book is based on a real transformation of a
village, Thenur from the state of poverty to
rehabilitation of villagers with basic healthcare needs,
job for adults and education for children; from the
state of frequent communal clashes and addictions to
the state of peace and prosperity)*

Published by
Jay Kay
writerjaykay@gmail.com

Powered by
Pothi.com
http://pothi.com

CONTENTS

PREFACE

PREFACE

Dear Readers,

'A Silent Revolution' is a book based on revelations of Mr. Senthil Kumar Gopalan a.k.a SKG, founder and president of the Payir Trust, Thenur, and Trichy

It is about a boy who has fulfilled his dream of Mahatma Gandhi's vision of 'Villages as the backbone of a country in a self-sustainable model

Today with over five thousand children have schools and hospitals for the entire community with free health care services for the poor with qualified physicians, and hospitals for the community savings live, and the de addiction centers helping youth

I had an opportunity to work with Mr. S.K.G in Troy, MI, USA. In his simplified style S.K.G used to quell about the dream of empowering villages...and his vision came true with his relentless hard work and dedication to the services

Here is a book based on the real life Hero 'Mr. S.K.G for his services towards humanity, who has proven strength, courage and sacrifices towards helping fellow human beings.

I salute our hero 'SKG'. A revolution has just begun!!!
The Author - Jay Kay

July 2013 CNN Hero 2013 Nomination

S.K.G was an I.T Consultant who had started his high flying career with IBM in niche areas with a very high pay in the MI, US in the year 1998-2005. Though he was working in the US, his heart and spirit was consistently dreaming about empowering a poor village in India with proper healthcare centers for all, education for young, and employment opportunities for adults to empower a family, a village on a whole. He decided to return back to India in 2004 permanently with all the money that he had earned, invested over $ 100,000 USD whatever savings he had.

S.K.G has invested his entire savings to start up a health care facility, school and home for poor despite all the hardships from the Government with absolute lack of support. He did not stop; he relentlessly worked towards building homes for the destitute, and a school for children.

Today after all the hardships with his forsaken personal interests, he was able to build up a poor village in a sustainable model with basic requirements of healthcare center, school and jobs for many adults. Thus, he transformed a poor village into a sustainable model in its micro economic model, poverty to success with smiles all around in thousands of family. It is truly commendable and a sustainable model in the rapid urbanization in every part of the World. His Organization called Payir trust is committed to empowering women, and children

PROLOGUE

As Mahatma said...

> *'Villages are the back bone of a Country'* as opined by Mahatma Gandhi

2005-2013 <u>PAYIR TRUST</u>

A transformation has begun with over a thousand household unanimously named the hero of the town known as the '**Thenur Shivaji**' meaning the savior of the land as Chatrapathi Shivaji of pre-Independent India.

Here is a real story of a Hero, a young entrepreneur who has sacrificed his professional career in the information technology working in the US, life for the welfare of the people, with a vision that is contemporary and beyond our times. Whilst our country is consistently failing to provide basic infrastructure, daunted with a failed democracy, and micro economy

The campaign of India shining is not true, until the tears of farmers are held. There are few people who campaign hard in the name of politics, and once they assume power…it will all be gone in the wind. Indeed a very few think about the backbone of India which is primarily made of villages, until the advent of technology which has made every villager to sell their lands and move to the cities with an ambition to make quick money or educate the children in engineering, medicine and technology etc.

The rapid urbanization has its benefits of creating more jobs, however on the flip side of total lack of interests in cultivating food. Hence, there is going to be an acute shortage of land and food in the upcoming years for the younger generations, unless villages are empower and self-sustainable model which would save the fate of the World in protecting villages against rapid urbanization and over population in cities, by providing required facilities to all. As Villages are as much as important as Cities, by providing basic health care for all, education for children and job for all, would create a micro-economy and a self-sustainable model by leveraging resources and wealth of the country

The idea seem to have gone into a boy with a vision of transforming a village, with the intense desire like a burning incense stick has sprout out to venture into a courageous venture of a trust called '**Payir Trust**', a non-profitable NGO which has the motto of human birth right to achieve a good quality life in every village with poorest of the poor enjoying the healthcare benefits, good education and jobs for adults like any other citizen in towns, and cities.

All of the above is not propaganda of another political party, which normally disappears after the election with the defaulting promises of the campaign. What is even more interesting is that the idea envisaged in a young mind has forged into a vision in a man, and the rest is what is known as the "Payir Trust", which is transforming a community in villages (7) in the district with a population of around 5000 men, women and children with half of these children are not in schools, which is even more alarming.

There is not a single hospital within 40 kms, which means there is no way to get emergency treatment whatsoever and the situation is even more worse with the infrastructure as they are depending on 1-2 buses that connects to the nearby towns. How many old men and women have died for no reason at all for the curse of the political parties which survive feeding themselves, instead of supporting the communities that are remote in the villages. Adding salt to the wound, there are interim communal clashes spiked up by the parties or whatever reasons it crops up every now and then, despite the state of affairs and the police force is busy escorting the top business men in the cities, and the coveted crowd of the ministers

Nor. Does the paparazzi team take a look except for the some men of movie venturing here every now and then for a movie song with the nice looking village background. God, would you give me two more hands with a bigger heart to serve till I live as SKG is praying hard is resounding in my ears as I speak

The man who has been crying by his heart and spirit, yearning for the liberation of these communities in the backyard of villages. If you close your eyes and imaging your kids playing with these poor children, there is no difference as GOD has designed everyone so unique. But the real problem relying in the economic disparity where in India, richer are getting to richest, and the middle class men are transforming themselves to the upper-middle class and find their way to the United states where they are foot loose, and fancy free for rest of their lives.

Nature has bestowed with everything...I believe these resources are not shared and education is primary as most of them are dying out of malnutrition is not acceptable...This is the root of our country, our heritage and my dear country men as I speak rise up to the occasion to support for a good cause.

Over two thousand children are being educated, homes for destitute, families are fed with jobs for adults with organic farming, hospitals and produce and computer education in villages which was nowhere in the agenda of any of the political party in India

The main goal of the farm is learn, develop and train villagers on new/traditional environmentally sustainable agricultural techniques. Currently we have a paddy plantation, a coconut grove and a garden of herbs.

We have started producing coconut compost within the farm; this is being used to fertilize the grove and garden. We hope to shortly make this available the villagers for them to use and sell.

The revolution has just begun as Mr. S.K.G who is known as the '**Thenur Shivaji'** in the community for his services. This is an example of exemplified courage, brilliance and micro-economy with self-sustainable model of a village in India, and the rest of the World. An ultimatum of a simple man with profound meaning of Payir Trust, with a vision of rural empowerment services for all

The vision is eternal as it has just started from a small village in India with a model that can be practiced anywhere in the World. While every graduate is hankering for a handsome salary in $$ for his own welfare with least botherations for the country, here is a man who comes for rescue. This man was once an IT Consultant worked in the US with a huge salary, and then returned back after five years with a vision to set up his community services in a village called Thenur in the southern part of India known as Trichy. The map portrays a village of extreme draught and conditions over a decade that has plunged the villagers into utter poverty and children malnourished

If you had fed the poor or treated the diseased, it would have been a short term endeavor. Instead Thenur Shivaji thought about the basic needs of every individual and the generations.

What is really saddening is that, often our country men forget themselves when they touch the shores of an alien country. They change, and behave like an alien which is predominantly the case in most of us behaving like a foreigner to our own country. More so you change your accent, behavior like an English man and thinking with no trace of heritage carrying over ten thousand years of wisdom and spirituality that you have inherited by Nature

It is like forsaking your mother for something else, the money which is the strong driving force behind everything. If not servicing the country, at least a least courtesy of thinking about uplifting the poor is required, to help alleviate the pains of the fellow human beings.

Needless to mention the selfless sacrifices of Annie Besant, and mother.Mirra those who were born in different countries had forsaken their personal interests for the welfare of the society. Mother Teresa had spent her entire life with the poorest of the poor, helping them transform. Each of them had brave hearts to transform addressing to the basic needs of humanity

The recent crime against women is due to lack of basic understanding of humanity; as even a least realization of people suffering around us would have transformed each of you…This is all due to the conditioning, and lack of realization

This is an ultimatum of truth to realize the values within each of you and help each other in promoting world peace by forming communities of self-reliant in every part of the world without barriers or boundaries

Payir is just a crop of truth in each of you. It will grow and spread itself in to the multitude of Universe across the shores in every part of the world. I will not stop until then, as the projects profile in Payir is ever growing for the humanitarian services from basic needs to the psychological and spiritual growth

It will bring the change in the next generation as you grow and observe things around you. Each of you will transform or help transforming children in the respective communities and the governance will change in the future. With all the impediments or challenges ahead will just wither away

A group of students asked Mahatma about the message for the young generations…

Mahatma replied 'My life is the message' and his entire life was his experiments of truth, guarded by the principles of Ahimsa and it extended beyond the shores of the country. Anything that a common man perceives is a universal property for the upliftment of the society on the whole.

The vision of Mahatma in transforming villages has forged in the young mind of S.K.G, who was fascinated by the Gandhian principles, and further his chronicle in the United States as a consultant had helped him build leadership skills, to identify problems suffocating the humanity at grass roots level.

The revelations of Mr. Thompson has guided him further into the next steps of setting up shores in India by sacrificing his professional and personal career for truth, in humanitarian grounds of serving the society

This story is about his life and the leadership that he has demonstrated despite several hiccups for the elite social cause

A Silent Revolution has just begun!!!
A Silent Revolution has just begun!!!

Let us be part of the Revolution with heart and spirit invoking the blessings for the ardent cause of PAYIR. A man who has started the revolution 2020 in creating awareness through the social media, with online advertisements with the network of over a million with some philanthropists who works more than sixteen hours day for fulfilling his dream, the ultimate dream of empowering villages.

As featured in one of the Tamil daily

newspaper..

*

Thenur Village Hospital

Inauguration Invitation
Thenur Village
Kunnam Taluk, Perambalur District

The people of Thenur village and The Payir Trust team cordially invite you to the Inauguration of the Thenur Village Hospital, a hospital built with the participation of the local village people.

Date:	December 5, 2006, Tuesday 12 noon India Time.
Chief Guest:	**Mr. Anil Meshram I.A.S.,** District Collector, Perambalur District
Presiding:	**Mr. K. Muthukkannu,** Chairman, Alathur Union
	Mr. C. Balakrishnan, M.A., B.Ed., Thenur Panchayat President
Special Address:	**Mr. S. Aiyyaru,** Project Officer, District Rural Development Agency
	Mr. A. Ramasamy, Project officer, Women's Development Project
	Dr. Thilakavathy, Joint Director, Health & Family Welfare
	Dr. Mohan, Deputy Director, Public Health
	Mrs. K. Sridevi, Chief Educational Officer
Welcome Song:	**Tamil Prayer Song**
Welcome Address:	**Mr. S. Sethuratnam.**

*

14

You were born together and together
you shall be for evermore
- Khalil Gibran.

*

Leader
Indeed Sun is the center;
Where all others would depend
There are leaders who give and take
Some would perhaps give!!!

There a very few who are real
Those who are part of the history
Like a sun they shine;

Finding this genius in a leader,
With his ardent smile he covers,
Perhaps leaders aren't born,
Made based on the occasion;

What is the purpose of leadership?
In the barricade of corporate functions;
The one who perceives your sufferings
Is a Christ Indeed;

Those who decide and find themselves
While discovering their path
Indeed, a rare species of Earth!
-    Jay Kay

One who has health has hope,
And the one who hope has everything!!!! – Arab proverb

Chapter 1 INSPIRATION 2013

"Vandhe Madharam", "Vandhe Madharam"

As the ringing tone calling for another freedom movement of this century….'S.K.G, wake up' it me Sam on the other end, a nerd in mid twenties was a bit restless just lying on his couch in the condominium in the city of New York.

It is a call from the Indian President's office for the Independence Day celebrations. Mm mm...Let me catch some sleep for few more minutes. Buddy, wake up. It is time to cherish as S.K.G kept mauling him down in the cell phone

What? What are you talking about?

Of course true. The president of India would like to present you an award. Your life will change forever.ok. Let's catch up. Will be ready in about 10. As he quickly refresh himself after the short Morning Prayer, with a modest breakfast of Raghi Dosa served with sambar provided by the Doctor. Giji. As the cat wags her tail in his bed 'meow' in the morning sun shine

Giji…stop serving this please. You are a doc. And above all chief of our hospital. Oh no. Mr. S.K, will need the president of the trust to keep his health to look after thousands of them

Excuse me. Hello Sir. This is something, the lead and a scientist and the President of India has arrived in his regular attire with the sparkling eyes wanting to discover more in space.

S.K.G wakes up a little late than usual due to the issues in the Organic farming, after carefully investigating the crops that have failed to produce and the drought conditions which has made the situations worse than ever. As he was reconciling his files to find out

I had a beautiful dream…where women and children are prosperous in the era of Golden times of India, where men were busy working in the field with the Elephant carts for plough their fields

In the rice bowl of South. India, Tanjore supporting the World in feeding millions of people. The dreams were growing larger and larger and the vision in my mind was clear to help in empowering the communities that need the most, and my way was to start from the grass roots.

I looked at the positive aspects of life. There are lots of things in the West, which I admired like their belief in their dreams and seeking a continuous improvement in their quality of life. The East is a comparatively mature society with respect to spiritual thought process. Similarly, a large section of the population has a wide knowledge on various subjects

While my heart feels for the disaster in Uttaranchal with the Tsunami effects of extreme monsoon and floods affecting the Himalayan dreams of several youth, our lack of disaster recovery is apparent and the houses constructed with no proper plan or as per the basic rules have proved to be a havoc. It is a disaster to the entire Nation, and the classical example of a failing democracy.

The Panchayati Raj system was implemented by British is a three-tier system in the state with elected bodies at the Village, Taluk and District levels. It ensures greater participation of people and more effective implementation of rural development programs. There will be a Grama Panchayat for a village or group of villages, a Taluk level and the Zillah Panchayat at the district level.

India has a chequered history of panchayati raj starting from a self-sufficient and self-governing village communities that survived the rise and fall of empires in the past to the modern institutions of Governance at the third tier provided with Constitutional support

Unfortunately there is a lot of work to empower these Panchayat Governance due to lack of good governance practices and supervising bodies, none of the plan gets implemented to support villagers, as a result the plight of children, and women continue even while India is termed as an IT corridor.

I was part of IBM in Chennai for a couple of years, before I transitioned as a Project Lead at Lason systems with an opportunity to managing large teams (30) in the Detroit, United States. It was an experience of project management and how tasks accomplished with proper planning and execution using tools, methods etc.

'Here you go Mr. Senthil Kumar Gopalan…..Gopaahaalan….the first glimpse of a young American lady pronouncing it a little differently'. I interrupted her quickly…"I am S.K.G from India;"

My first day was filled with excitement to find the huge infrastructure, corporate buildings in the big beaver road, large grocery stores, and medical care. I was asked to fill out the Social Security Number application as I did and waited in the office. It was my turn, in few minutes the lady staff had asked few questions and then my SSN was ready. She said it would be mailed to me.

'Here you go. You are all set Mr.SKG. You would receive a mail in next couple of days'

I was playing back in my memory. A few years ago back home in India:

'Why do you need an International Driver License? Sir. I am going to the United States. Is it so...where is your visa and the ticket? Sir...here it is

The Inspector checks the documents

Sare sare. Yellam sariya errukku!

Edhavathu donation kuduthuttu poh thambi...what?

As was shocked? To whom should I donate and for what? I have all the documents, and my flight ticket etc.

Thambi. Listen! There are ways followed since the post Independent era. This is how our judicial system works. Just do it or get out of here without a license issued.

Pay couple of thousand rupees and move on, as I have other clients.

Sir. Sir. As I requested. As I did not have that much money to pay him as I counted the bills...it was short of a thousand rupees and handed over whatever I had

"Get out. I am not a Security Guard" ok. I will not forward your application to the Chief Inspector for the approval and license. Get lost.

I was really lost in this event as I wanted every human right to be followed and for a simple reason breaking rules is not acceptable in a great democracy like in India as I thought and left the place with resentment....

*

I was thinking about the Panchayat offices and the lack of governance practices back home. I believe the term village is a colonial term indicating the rural area. Every area in the United States wherever you go was well connected to the cities with the basic needs fulfilled anywhere in the United States. This was amazing to me, when I compare the state of India. There are few towns around that are serene, peaceful such as SLC, UT which are well connected.

One thing that I observed was transparency in the US Governance. Or perhaps the awareness levels were quite high amongst the citizens of the country. No wonder US is termed as the best country in the World due to its robust Governance and policies that would reach individuals

Further, I did analyze little bit about the constitution framework and what makes them stand apart from rest of the World:

I had an opportunity to attend the Constitution class room sessions for couple of days to understand the American Constitution framework.

Johanna was our instructor…

She was discussing various facets of the American economy and the basic constitutional framework

As I asked her

Hi Johanna,

S.K.G as I called as in elsewhere…what is your question

Who is the supreme power of the constitution framework as she explained the 'Congress' which can turn the president down? Hence, the system is not just a one man army; instead it is primarily governed by the congress. The house and senate have prime responsibilities in the Federal Governance. You might have heard about presidents have been impeached by the House of Representatives (Andrew Johnson and Bill Clinton), neither of them was removed following trial in the Senate.

*

The Real Democracy- United States

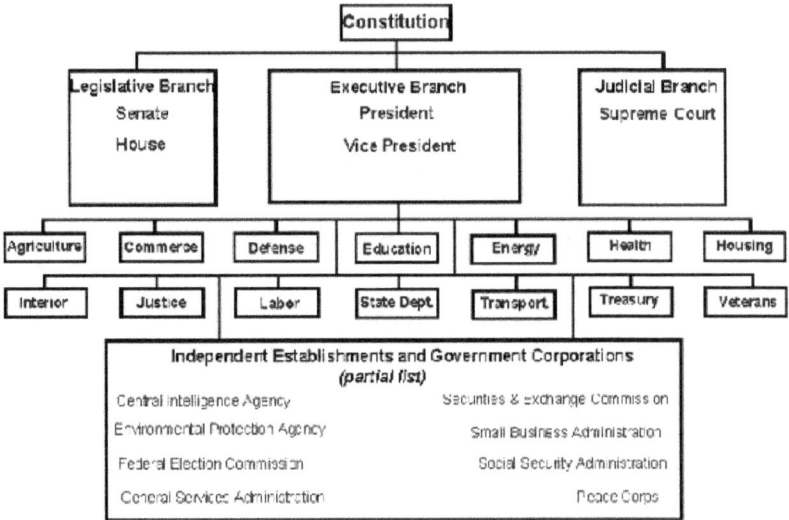

It is simple and a transparent framework with the President, Senate and the Supreme Court with Federal, State Governance of fifty states. The United States Congress is the legislative branch of the federal government. It is bicameral, comprising the House of Representatives and the Senate, who abide by the congressional procedures

I was astonished to hear that US State Congress is more powerful, including power to remove the President of United States as I studied further in greater details of Governance structure. In simple terms state and federal are synonymous to the state and central in India There are 435 representatives, each of whom represents a congressional district.

There are two senators from every state (50) and the senate election is every two years. The House and Senate each have particular exclusive powers. For example, the Senate must approve (give "advice and consent" to) many important Presidential appointments, including cabinet officers, federal judges (including nominees to the Supreme Court), department secretaries (heads of federal executive branch departments), U.S. military and naval officers, and ambassadors to foreign countries. All legislative bills for raising revenue must originate in the House of Representatives.

The approval of both chambers is required to pass any legislation, which then may only become law by being signed by the President (or, if the President vetoes the bill, both houses of Congress then re-pass the bill, but by a two-thirds majority of each chamber, in which case the bill becomes law without the President's signature). The powers of Congress are limited to those enumerated in the Constitution; all other powers are reserved to the states and the people.

In short a great Nation like US is able to implement a simple and transparent Governance model in its constitution by the way of forming Federal and State which are synonymous to the Indian system of Central and State. However, the Governance varying in Himalayan terms and context

As I thought, I'd like to compare the constitution of India and where do we lack in terms of Governance, and transparency. I believe our India constitution was framed with the base model of that of British model of parliamentary democracy.

When the plans were concrete, however the sufferings of human beings brought the conditions in my mind, as I realized. It happened to me too..

These are the points that I captured for a better governance, looking at the robust procedures and the constitutional framework and lot of things to revise or perhaps amend in the Indian constitution for a better India as I thought by the end of the session

Troy is an affluent city in Oakland County in the U.S. state of Michigan, and is a suburb of Detroit. I was driving at I-75 from Troy, MI with the population of less than a lakh, to a nearby town Sterling Heights appx. About 50kms from Troy. It is a beautiful place with orchards near the woods park, as I spent my time over a weekend whenever I want to contemplate my goals, reading the vision of Swami Vivekananda.

Whenever I crossed the Troy Union cemetery; I stopped for a while looking at each of those quiet ones, as the pigeon poking each of their hats of silent men around who had reached the peak of the corporate regime. As it implied me something, perhaps someone wants to hint at me by saying..Hey you look here for what you are? The real one, just face-off.

It was summer; as the entire Michigan state was rejoicing warmth of the sun shine, as often we get a lot of snow, storm and cold weather most of the year; as I drove thinking deep in to my consciousness; a sudden experience!
'Where am I? As the envision of a young man with confidence intruding me

My Spiritual Encounters
A tall person with long hair, white beard in his white Indian attire of someone closer to my heart as I was trying to look through my mind for his name; couldn't see him though, as the fog was obstructing my vision. It was a Yogic experience

I am your angel as he replied. My dear friend what are you doing here in this country? I'll show you something…he continued, perhaps I have been trying to find you since you were there at a young age

Perhaps. You are deep in sober. What are you up to. Did you find the answers? My brothers and sisters are suffering. As I looked closer in his eyes filled in tears, perhaps tears of post war trauma, as I kept witnessing him. There were over thousands of them, men and women and children who were crying and seeking help. Some old men were diseased and the vision was through his eyes. And each of them were drowning in to a dark sea and I could feel and hear the voice seeking help…It's me help me bro!

The vision had lasted for less than couple of minutes, but profound and left me in to a state for a while. Sir. I don't understand you? Who are you? As I kept my inquisitiveness.

You know me. You have been talking to me in the orchard, and back at the garden restaurant when you and I met second time

It was a vision or dream or real as time in continuum cannot tell as I am looking for answers. It is reminiscent in my memories as I tried to recollect my instances of any such experiences of the past. Finally, he disappeared and never had a chance to meet him again.

These spiritual encounters are possible, if you are aligned to a subtle state of mind as I took the exit back home and parked my vehicle

*

Jay "It is true my life has been a journey. Evolving from the mundane to the revolution. Often times God finds someone to talk to, and he chooses some messages to be passed on to you specifically couriered to you to drive beyond mundane plane of life.

J: 'I hear that' as I walked away still thinking about his vision and experiences

J: 'I reckon there was a strong message delivered to you'

"Often time you do not feel achieving something if you are endowed in routine tasks; until the day you find certain extraordinary experiences which happened to me"

As I continued interrupting with all my questions

Of course. Each of these messages could not have been delivered if I were not receptive. I contemplated in some aspects of humanity perhaps…to help the poorest and it was not a campaign in my mind, perhaps to give them an opportunity for young children

Interrupted by the ring tone…'Vandhe Mataram…Vandhe Mataram' The irony is that our country men will turn in to unity in a major disaster where the humanity is felt, and the freedom struggles has yielded in tremendous leadership in India.

As I picked up the phone..

'This is Krish, from the President's office. We would like to present you an award of humanity for the community services'

Be there one hour at around 7 AM, as the morning at the National High School, Trichy. Ok.

I was not expecting this, as I thought is this a hoax? Someone playing prank…but what followed in a day was a package delivered by the Government of India…The welcome kit announced the award and the formalities. Which will be presented by the president of the country?

Am I going to meet the President, which was in my dreams. Is this all real and true as I exclaimed

'It is real as I insisted on the present events of significance and reality'

Jay, I can't believe this would help me extend wings in every village in India, isn't?

Over 700,000 of them and you have all the liberty to do so if you need one more life-time, will pray to God as I exclaimed!!!

Jay…what about the opportunities to visit Africa. Let me talk to the President for the campaign overseas, as I nodded my head with apprehension as SKG is already spending 16-18 hours a day!!!

Thambi,…sappad ready as I overheard with the giggling stomach feeling the sensations of hunger. A long and nice plantain leaf, with the first servings of rice and sambar, with the tingling pickles and rasam.

As I enjoyed the sumptuous meal, ending with the sweet payasam (deserts) I thoroughly enjoyed…

As we continued in the next morning….As I assembled in the Payir's next vision of Organic farm. How did you come up with this idea of the Organic farming…

Well. While I was in the US, I found Organic produce was common and people had started funding these projects due to the artifacts of deadly diseases such as Cancer linked to the pesticides used in the inorganic farming which is our current farming all over in India. Unarguably US government has banned in most of the villages in the US, however some companies have started exporting it to the Asian countries. This would result in deadly diseases ,as I fear. Have you heard about GM seeds?

J:Oh my God. Never heard of that. What does GM indicate?

S: Jay, it indicates 'Genetically Modified' when you change the genetically without knowing its harmful effects, it is like playing with Nature without knowing it.

I hear that…

To create awareness, I have simple and profound ways of Organic produce in our farms. This will earn regular income for the villagers with a plan to distribute vegetables through the society farm at a reasonable price, and it will extend to agriculture and dairy products

Hmmm..Interesting. Did you know in some countries they inject cattle, and they mix chemics to the cattle feed to increase milk production

I see. This is dangerous and I am not what will happen to the future generations

S: Jay..Not to scare you indeed. To help you understand and the harmful effects of nuclear radiation..

Of course true. I have been hearing about the nuclear reactors of sub-standard material which is rather more dangerous to our country, especially with poor disaster recovery management

Look at the Tsunami, and a nuclear disaster in Japan. And they are planning to generate electricity with Wind mill operations, furthermore they would stop nuclear reactors in phases. The same is true in the US too, with elections campaign for clean environment.

Why are we buying the dumped goods from the overseas? Perhaps there is a political gain, who knows? Unless you get in to the electoral campaign

J:Why don't you get into the Panchayat elections

S: Of course. I would like to contest as I can do more ..

Very good. Our country needs people like yourself who are visionary, young leaders who can empower youth and you have proved your abilities and I do not think anything else would be required beyond the sacrifices what you've done

S.K.G Kumar G 'You are the best countrymen…'

S.K.G: 'Common Jay. Don't be formal. It is our responsibilities as I thought what have I done for the country except blaming someone for all the failures?'

'SKG has not changed a bit in become even more simpler as I thought..from the office days. In fact spirited deeply rooted in his consciousness with a determination of a lion-heart to empower villages'

True. True. By the way how is the IT market treating you nowadays?

'The competition is increasing, consulting opportunities with specialist skills are more as you have seen in the US. There is a lot of consulting opportunities here .I do see tons of students from Korea, Africa around studying IT, Business in Bangalore'

I feel honored to hear that…

However..the stress levels has increased with number of diabetic youngsters is a common sight due to work related stress, and lack of spending time with the family

Oh no.

There were not more than top 10 IT companies in the 90's, and it has gradually increased with every top tier clients such as IBM, GE, Accenture, Cognizant, Vodafone and many more have operations extended to the shores of India

I guess Delivery centers are doing well, employing thousands of young entrepreneurs, and engineers. It is a good sign of our economy providing jobs in the first place, though we should strive for product development, rather than the consulting services alone.

My only fear is that the economy should provide some equality without hiking up commodities which is creating an imbalance in the country between the top IT vs. non IT professionals. If this trend continues, there will be a lot of vacancies in other departments, which is not a good sigh. We need to be balanced with appropriate tax structure with equal opportunities in every sector

I have to opine. I was a Mechanical Engineer turned into the Information Technology consulting. Nevertheless now ended up in a different career

I was excited about the infrastructure, township planning and the down-town. Often wondered why we are far behind in achieving feats of success. Though, most of you would say it is because of population, what happened to Singapore which is more populated / SQ.KM with the entire size of country smaller than Karnataka. Well. If it is possible for Singapore, India can also build up integrity and governance that can sustain. We need Government organizations, and MNC's to implement the best techniques in agriculture to help in organic farming

It depends on each of you, those who are dreaming about India a country which was once the Golden age where there was no evolution of Human in other parts of the world, India had the enlightened saints based of ardent inner engineering practices and discipline. I cherish the success of our inner world and the culmination of human consciousness has evolved, where east and west will join hands with each other

The global economy will improve and the macro finances would be common as we are largely become dependent with goods and services shipped from India, China reaching the shores of the United States, and the authors, and actors of the western world becoming a household name in the East. There is a true statement that 'world has shrunk'. There is no point in thinking antagonistic about anyone or idealism, the conflicts in idealistic principles can be resolved through intellectual reasoning and science which can demystify everything with one common Religion and world governance

The basic needs of humanity are the same regardless of caste, creed and religion and it cannot be different as NATURE has bestowed each of with the same water to drink and food to eat. Perhaps the minds are conditioned and it thinks different, however the purpose of life is to reach the sublime and the ultimate consciousness. You are born intelligent with success if you would listen to the language of heart, but conditioned by the society and various other factors thus attributing you for failure

The civilization evolved and has reached to the peak, first time our consciousness is evolving and it has to reach the peak to avert any mass destruction. The nuclear weapons have reached many countries, if someone uses it in an emotional state of Mind. It will be the end of the world

Let's build the universal brotherhood and realize the sacrifices and services rendered by great Mahatma's of the world. Your heart would melt in devotion. I am not saying you should sacrifice for the welfare of the society. Just streamline yourself first, family and then help each other whichever way it is possible.

The poverty is one of the basic problems in India due to uneven economics, and political in the World largest democracy daunted with plague called corruption. Hence the Government schemes, policies are often drained perhaps, without reaching the poorest of the poor. As an end result it denies proper education for children who would continue with the same fate of their parents, and the sufferings never end

There was a phase during the year **2005-2010**, where many farmers in Andhra Pradesh had committed suicide due to the loans repayment, and it continued in several parts of the country due to drought conditions and inclement weather everywhere. India is a country of Agriculture, as our country men had the production of food, poultry and dairy products as the predominant industry from time immemorial. With the rapid Industrialization during pre-Independent India under the British Raj, and Globalization post the Indian Independence have changed the fate of India for good and bad.

The situation is that many MNC's have set up shores in India in the name of Globalization with offshore divisions sprouting out every year for utilizing the services, the basic needs of human in villages seem to be a distant dream, and there is a saying in Tamil language:

> *"The one who farm*
> *Is the one who has just a handful?"*

The basic economics should treat each of the citizens with inequality with a fair basic facilities provided for all. If a country is not able to provide fair economics, then the country is disparate in its economy and has no business in the world economy. It is a shame rather than claiming India's success stories

Ask what you have done for the country? The answer is the heads down as the situation is that every Indian is feeling proud carrying the 'Green Card' and/or H1-B1 visas which seems to be the only talk of the town

It is up to the individuals; however the fact is that how of many you even think about giving it back to the society. I admire a great Nation such as US, at the same time I am happy to be an Indian simply for the heritage that we inherit. Needless to portray the boundaries of India just by the landscape, the country has much more to offer in spirituality

Trust in my Mind

The Payir Trust was formed in difficult times when there was no sponsorship, investing his hard earned money for forming the trust, and funds were utilized for the construction of the hospital. An outpatient health center with 2 beds, a laboratory and a dispensary has been successfully completed. The health center currently provides first aid, but will be shortly enhanced to provide primary health care. Literally he was on the cross roads, as there was no support from the local Government, except for few well-wishers and sponsors for some of the colleagues in the US, he was managing to run the NGO with available funds.

In due course he transformed this into a self-sustainable model, and self-reliable without having to look for the funding alone, which is not only the source of finances as the Organic farming, Agriculture, produce & dairy farm helped in building the corpus for sustainability in a micro-economic model first ever in the history of India, and the World .This is one of the endeavors that every single Governments have failed to eradicate poverty and help villagers to be sustainable

The Payir Trust is a beginning, which is a beginning of a new rural empowerment plan which is pragmatic and self-sustainable, which can be followed anywhere in the World. It is an example of exemplified services to the humanity by providing education for over a thousand children in the community

It is a means of expressing your joy. The joy of giving it back to the society, that has helped you grow. You give back to the society supporting its fundamental dynamics of the economy. The Payir trust, a renowned NGO in the region is not just feeding a community, perhaps transform it courageously what governments have failed to accomplish in over fifty years of freedom, and independence.

Payir is just a beginning of a revolution against poverty to provide the basic necessities to all humans, where a real democracy will blossom with individuals having a chance to reach the glory of humanity to grow spiritually. It is a beginning of a radical change in the way you think about the villages, where the paradigm shift would take every village to the World Globally!

Payir did not want to empathize their conditions by providing food for all or a common minimum programme as a short-term and/or one-time endeavor. Perhaps Payir has transformed thousands of individuals to support them from the basic needs, thus transforming an individual, a family and a community to the whole. The power, courage and strength had come to Mr. S.K.G, who is an ardent follower of Swami Vivekanda

It was imminent during my days that I had spent with him, who was constantly visualizing his vision and the power of thought has come true with the forging truth for humanity

The humanity is continue to evolve by some good human beings, whilst corrupt politics continue to swindle away wealth from the Individuals, here is a contemporary human who has elevated fellow human beings. As I regard this to be the highest service of the humanity.
As saint.Vallar said…

Food for all was one of the virtues of his philosophy

And Mahakavi Bharti has opined:

> *'Destroy the whole World*
> *If there is no food for even*
> *One being anywhere in the World"*

As Swami Vivekanda opined…

> *'India my land of spirituality*
> *Where its people are Spiritual'*

Perhaps you have forgotten the simple language of the heart and love. Since you have been diagnosed with the 'diabetic-mellitus' as I'd often call, which is nothing but money. By now you would have realized that money cannot buy happiness but everything else. You seem to be carrying that a lot in every moment of your life as your ambition…Swami Vivekananda's ambition was globalizing thoughts of 'Vedanta' not to propagate Hinduism. Indeed it was west and the Moghul kingdom has imposed isms into India. India has always been defeated in several wars by the British, Portuguese, and the Moghuls for centuries as it hankered for only one thing. 'Peace.'

In the chronicles of Parahamsa Yogananda, and Sri.Baba you would find heritage of your own culture and the country. Instead of teaching the best of virtues, you seem to be denying it vehemently submerging yourself into the Western worlds. From time immemorial, India had the enlightened souls for centuries in Buddha, Sankara, Siddhas' etc. These are the greatest souls of wisdom who have had the intelligence of Einstein with the only difference of theory vs. revelations, where they had the revelations of truth. The cosmic consciousness and it was natural to finding the truth in the evolution on human consciousness. While our endeavor has extended beyond shores in touching frontiers of East and the West with the rapid Globalization shrinking the economy in the history of evolving human consciousness

From time to time Nature is sending in its prophecies of truth in saviors of truth, these are the truth cops who are rebellious to bring the metamorphosis in the human consciousness external or internal where the socio-economic factors are considered. In the form of

Swami Vivekanda who is an ardent seeker of Spirituality propagating wisdom of truth as 'Vedanta' with the first ever speech of a Hindu monk in Chicago which has its own significance

With the evolution of many spiritual seekers in India, India has always known for its vibrant seekers of truth, and the achievers who are the realized souls such as Vethathiri of this century with profound wisdom of the 'Unified Force' aligned with Einstein's Theory of Relativity with axioms based on his revelations. There were several other seers such as Yogananda Parahamsa who is known in the West, saint. Boghar who could transform his ethereal body; All of it is on the spiritual plane of life, whereas during the freedom period there were great poets such as Mahakavi Bharti who had tremendous wisdom, and insights in terms of several revolutionary poetry to create awareness amongst youth of the nation. Some of his poetries were ahead of his time...such as this

'Even the crows and sparrows belong to my caste; Whilst, the mountains, and oceans belong to my species;'

The above poetry indicates the biological functions of crows and sparrows compared to human beings, and the inanimate nature of five elements is similar to that of human beings. Indeed true, the forgotten language s of a great country posts the free-India. The land called Bharat is often misinterpreted as poor.

*"Is there any dearth of wealth in India?
In the Eastern Himalayas to the
West of Bay of Bengal"*

With the landscape and perfect climatic conditions, India can do Agriculture all around the year and suitable for Industrialization without impacting the schedule due to any extreme weather in most part of the India

Nature has cast a play as it felt the pressure of human consciousness suffering as a savior Mahatma who had come to free India. In a similar term S.K.G has been transformed to Shivaji of Thenur. An incredible warrior pre-Independence era of Indian independence.

SKG was able to transform a village with over thousand households below the poverty line to a self-sustainable model in the history. The Government of India has not been able to provide basic necessities to every Indian as they look at the election campaign beyond humanity. This is a model that can set an example to UNESCO (UNO) to support in every country to empower the villages. The rural empowerment was a concept of an emerging economy, and it is not required to relocate everyone to the cities Why is that every village is financially backward as I traced the roots of villages to find a definite answer within self after investigating few villages in AP and TN, wherein the cities have expanded beyond the limits of IT corridor with poor infrastructure, funding to build the villages.

Even today there are a lot of villages in India without proper hospitals, schools to support and jobs for adults. As a result, they live in absolute poverty and children with being educated turn out to be criminals of the future. As Mahatma opined…Today's Youth are the leaders of tomorrow!!! Isn't that required to build a country from the basic foundation of education for children those who are poor, and the destitute who need required care which is perhaps the principles of real democracy and the World largest democracy has failed to take care of the back bone of our country. As a result there is a rapid urbanization and people shifting their locations to the cities searching for jobs and the children are just the caretakers, and babysitters of the contemporary society. Where they are abused, tortured in the cities with the lowest pay and living condition to make the condition worse

If a village suffers, a state will suffer and the country will suffer on a whole. If a country is inadequate to take care of the basic necessities of its people, there is no reason to feel proud of anything, Indeed it is a failed democracy and the state affairs are just a mockery despite being the largest Nation with several millions working all over the world. In a true sense, it is rather a shame than proud to honor the tricolor which has worsened the conditions post-Independence.

In every election campaign, there have been promises that were made of the upcoming roads, hospitals, schools and colleges and jobs for adults with ray of hopes for over a thousand household. This was never meant to be true as the calendar days reckon the hopes turning shadows of instances with no development whatsoever, and whosoever becomes the Prime Minister. The situation of a small village, Thenur remained in the political map of India with no further development. The history of more than three decades of drought conditions have made the entire community weaker with no hopes of rehabilitation with the staggering number of people relocation from village to the nearby towns and cities for any kind of jobs.

Title: The Shivaji of Thenur

Before the aged men, and women of the retired farmlands have been looking agape facing up to the heaves and clouds to shower, year after year, and the prayers of religious sentiments in the small temple in the village with the mother. Goddess listening to the state of affairs. Perhaps the call was made in heavens with Nature taking charge of the state of affairs, with the deafening words into ears of Politicians, hence the savior came in *'__The Shivaji of Thenur__'*…who is the man on the field passionately named by the villagers, who had the humungous task of resolving the conflict in the region; a small village known as Thenur in Trichy, Tamil Nadu.

Thus, a silent revolution had started in the village which has the blueprint of a success from the village of Thenur. It is just the beginning of a revolution, and the Nature's cast is now Globalizing the society in the peak of human consciousness.

One of the objectives of Payir is to transcend beyond villages to empower the communities, from the Thenur to Africa. A contemporary IT Gandhi of our times, who is a legend with forsaken interests of selfless desires to empower every village in the World, and empower every community in the World

While I was reading Mahatma's 'My Experiments of Truth' here is an IT Mahatma of our times, who has had very little interests of his self. With his desires of truth extending beyond the boundaries, and the wings of wisdom touching shores of everywhere communities are crying for help

It is an intimate cast of mother. Nature in Payir, and S.K.G who is an avatar of our times with the expanded consciousness extending his desires of eternity in empowering every community.
Let us join hands in helping Payir a world Organization for rural empowerment, and wish him over hundred years to empower villages in every part of the World. Every individual, especially youth are pride to carry the vote of thanks without identifying the electoral responsibilities

More so, those who are from the roots of villages are even shying away to name the background with a pride remark of an English accent with keys to driving Honda's which still remains the passion for a mundane mind. Whilst so, here is a gentleman who has sacrificed his well-being for the welfare of the society

I often visited the Benihana restaurant for lunch in the Big Beaver road…it was always a warm welcome with the traditional Japanese shushi that I enjoyed to the core along with a few of my colleagues who loved Chinese, and Japanese food especially sizzling shrimp and red lobster with rice remains my favorite food till date.

Back in my homeland there were simple and profound experiences that had touched my heart through the angels of heart from the paradise. One such personality is AAnjamma.

Today I visited a person who is nearing 80. She has done yeoman service in her professional life spanning nearly 50 years and still doing in other ways. During our conversation, at one point she told that she is surprised that I carry the hope for a better to-morrow. She says, with the magnitude of (immoral) happenings that she sees around today, people (like her) of her generation hope only for the end of their mortal life. I am sure, this is not one person's commentary, but of many.
This strikes me very hard. If our generation is creating such disdain with our previous one, we need to question ourselves what is that we are giving to our next generation?

I tell myself that all these stuff of working for social development is secondary, tertiary more so...the most important meaningful work we can do ..Is to create HOPE...a hope that communities and societies based on compassion, honor and truth can exist even among the ruins created by the same human society.

I met him after almost a decade though we were in touch through the internet and the social media. These days of wisdom have made him stronger with a lion heart to face and lead the world by his presence with a vision in his eyes, and words ceaselessly flowing through the mind as usual with his simple and profound etiquette of humanity touching several lives of thousands of the villagers...those who claim him as the 'Kaval Theivam' meaning the Savior and the king of the poorest of the poor and an Emperor of the wises ones

SKG's ideals were different from others as he was holistic in his views as he spoke to me while we were in the US about the projects in a humble way...

'I have chosen Sathanoor as my starting place due to it being my mother's home village; the knowledge of the people; the environment and the fertility of the land. My grandmother lives in the village and has about 3-4 acres of land. There is also a huge home. If possible I will try to convince my grandmother and my maternal uncles to start managing the farm. If not, my 1 Lakh reserve will be used to buy and cultivate a small piece of land. My personal requirements are very minimal with a small place to live and the food from the farm. I will not keep a saving for myself, as I am against insurance of myself in this endeavor. The income from the farm should take care of my livelihood as well as some of the requirements for the project.

My financial commitment and commitment by way of blood relationship to my family, is limited only to my parents. Before I left India for greener pastures, I was determined to help them self-sustainable as it my responsibilities. They had managed my upbringing so well in the past, so I have no doubts that my parents have already decided my commitment to the ir future is redundant. Anyhow, knowing my family, in case of necessity, my brother and sister would be always there to help and take care in every manner, when I cannot. As far as my siblings and their family, I will be detached and my commitment is only moral support.

The determination of a teenager has gone deep in the consciousness as stated below. He was determined to marry a handicapped person…as some men in India should feel ashamed of seeking dowry for marrying a bride. What a shame. If you are young men? Think about it…Let's not defame the state of women please.

I may or may not get married. If I were getting married, my wife would be a person who will support this cause. If possible, I would like to marry a handicapped person.'

Nature had its plans to find a beautiful bride for SKG whom he met while deep in love as much as the PAYIR organization with the blossoming love to find his life partner in Preeti…

Did you observe the visions as I read through his mind several years after he said almost a decade and every word of his virtues have come true? It is a real witness of how thoughts forging into actions, if it were for real and good purpose. Each and every step that he took was observed by Nature and the support came from the cosmic consciousness as the 'Fraction demands and the totality supplies'

At one point in this endeavor he was advised by a retired Doctor who has wealth of experience in setting up the health care centers to limit the construction of hospital to a 2 bed hospital. Which he apparently denied as his vision was at least a 10 bed hospital to support over 3000 villagers in and around Thenur village, as emergencies cannot be always handled to Trichy hospitals and some of his childhood memories of Vijaya ma...have forged his convictions. The real convictions to help poorest of the poor

Ethics of Payir

I had observed the transparency and honesty in the United States in every wake of life with business code as principles from a grocery store to the Target stores and the government offices. The US constitution has reached the masses of helping its citizens as it takes care of every individual with the social security fund so on...and so forth, with every town well connected to the cities with the forests preserved and awareness about pollution and recycling etc. amongst the elevated individuals. Hence, in my later stages of forming Payir, I wanted a process driven approach with code of principles with transparency especially in spending money obtained by the way of charity. The district collector who is an ardent follower of Mahatma Gandhi came forward with all the support

This was a blessing in disguise to support provided by the Government officials.

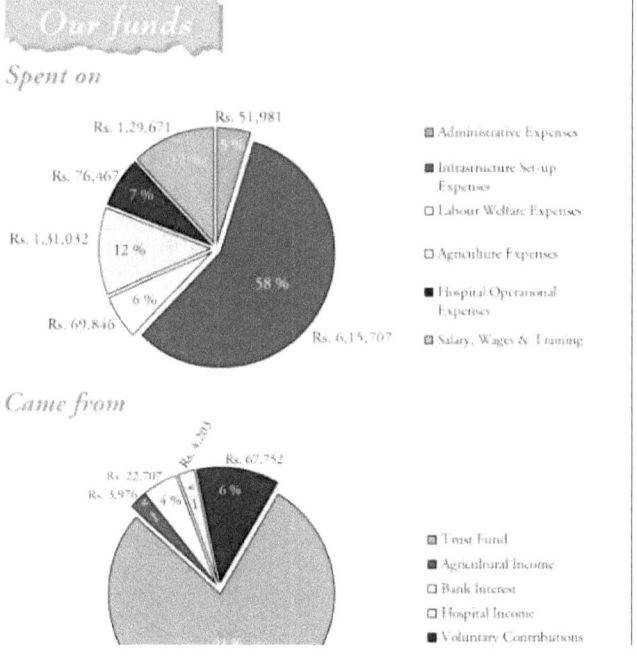

The funds and every dime to the chime as we call it perhaps was spent meticulously for the welfare and it was measured accurately with the chart of accounts managed by SKG. The above graph indicates PAYIR's spending with excellent governance to ensure its

sustainability with a vision of long term. There was no room for errors or scope of any invalid spending's as the system was robust

*

2010 – Interview with Vijay TV.
I received a call from the Vijay TV marketing office indicating their interest to publish Payir and interview me...I said 'Is that true?' as often actors get the prominence in India from the commercial ad's to the political campaign or a cricket star, as I exclaimed within myself!!!

'Sir..Neenga next Monday ready a erunga' be ready by next Monday for a 2 hours session as Vijay TV had indicated....

Well. TV, camera and lights on..I didn't do any make-up as I was busier than ever teaching small children. The discussion started from the organic farm (coconut), to the questions about my work in the US...

I answered all of them in one take and the session was over. Thanks to Vijay TV as there was an overwhelming responses from the viewers with several emails, messages and blogs praising me!!!

I just thought...don't need anyone to praise me. If possible just support others through the possible ways that you can!!!!

Chapter 2 THE BIRTH OF PAYIR

Payir meaning a "crop" that which you sow is what you would reap!!! Payir is sowing seeds. The seeds of soul with the goal to fulfill basic needs of every individual, with a holistic development of everyone, especially the villages those who do not have the basic needs fulfilled.

The communities should be self-reliant and sustainable which was not the case when I enquired with some of the localities.

Any community should be able to own the ideas that are needed for their continuous development — be it their physical, civic or spiritual. Owning of the ideas means collectively create new thoughts and create/manage resources to implement and execute it. At the individual level, each individual should be able to self-realize his/her own potentials, without any distinction based upon caste or creed. This would in essence mean to build an environment where even the most ordinary person lives with self-respect.

As the memories of my childhood reminiscent in myself…My pre-school years were mainly spent in my mother's village, Sathanoor. I joined school at the age of six the first standard (no kindergarten) at Pennadam Sugar Factory where my father worked as a factory cashier. Later, to provide better education to us children (I have an older sister and an older brother), my mother shifted to Tiruchi, while my dad used to visit us during the weekends.

From the third standard till 10th I studied in Sri Akilandeshwari Vidyalaya very close to my home in Mambalasalai. During this time, I was a carefree boy…playing cricket or chess. I did decently well in studies, coming within the top five in my class. Then, I did my higher secondary at R.S. School, BHEL. This was the period where I started sharing and discussing my thoughts to give it concrete shape.

I contemplated on the business plan to start off from the grass roots to venture in to supporting human consciousness. If it is collecting a fund for the welfare of humanity, we do not know how it is being spent in projects, as I have my doubts in the governance of

NGO's, I wanted to implement effective measures to change the way we think, a radical approach in holistic empowerment of humanity. You cannot expect a poor man suffering from diseases, or dying out of hunger to grow spiritually. It has to start from fulfillment of basic needs as I have witnessed propriety in the United States where they tend to have a different problem. At least not the daunting problems of hunger and survival; The basic needs are well taken care of in Social Security funds for all, with the food prices are at the lowest, and everyone could afford for a car as a default. I was even more astounded to find the sanitary engineers driving best vehicles. There aren't too many rag pickers as I talked to one of them.

From Troy, United States to Thenur, India

For me, career is not tied to one technology and Surely not based on success on one particular area of work. Looking back, I started my work in a sugar factory. Though my assignment was management trainee, my learning over there was not on technology, but on mentoring; people's thought process in rather mundane job like running a crusher, fork-lift crane operation, sugar sampling – all of which I performed. Later when I joined the Thermal Power plant, I learnt and applied on the job, one of mechanical engineering's best subjects. My real learning though was, compassion at work, expediency of life services (just think of tripping the plant, would mean black out in Bombay and cascading effect to the Western grid), working with tribal and culture. In both these jobs, I was considered (with all my humbleness!) as the brightest new face in that industry. IBM taught me "Process" and Lason, Project management and cross-culture behavior.

I intercepted an Old man on my way back from work in Troy, finding him in extreme cold. Shivering. thought of helping him. It was a long winter with beautifully decorate light amidst soft white snow with children playing with the soft snow ball...and few youngsters were skating wild adventurous to watch under lights.

The ice-skaters were busy in the competition with MI Warriors vs. Chicago bulls. It was a match that my colleague wanted to watch for months.

My Intimate Conversation

I slowed down at lights turned to halt me. I paused my car music aloud in the Christina's songs. I just peep out of the window as I opened my foggy power window of the Honda Civic sedan...Hi there...can you hear me?

Hi bud "hi you there" An old man shivering in cold with torn coat which was not caring for winter...

Isn't there a Christmas around the corner? And what are you doing here as mulled across picking up a fallible conversation, as I thought it is rather easier to start conversing with light minded person...who was looking to rest and dose off instantly

I shook his hands a little more firmly. How do you do Sir?

He was a little embarrassed for a stranger wishing him…

Well. I am fine. How long have you been here?

I am Mr.Jones Thompson

Well Mr. Thompson. I am S.K.G K, "**S.K**.G". How long have you been here?

It's about fifty years. He looked confident with sparkling eyes.

Here is my coat. Just be comfortable. I can offer you a ride.

A little perturbed. I am fine Mr.S.K.G

I took him to the nearest Café Day for a cup of coffee

Mr.S.K.G. I have been living in this country for three decades now. This is what I have chosen

Where are you originally from?

I am from South Africa. Haunted by the civil war and lost my family. Just hanging in here

I was a business man...diamond business with billions of dollars earned

I had few diamond factors in the suburbs of Seorro Leone…which was all destroyed in a coup attempt and my family was confiscated; and with the support of my friends, I boarded the ship to New York.

I looked his traces of sadness in his brown eyes and the nerves were string like showing his resentment towards someone…

Well. I didn't want to work thought my friends had insisted me on starting up my diamond business. I had no reason. Nothing much except surviving

I believe in God protecting me and there is a reason for my survival as I felt after several years in trauma. And then I had a dream...

God talked to me. Of course it was him with the soft white light surrounding and the path to the heaven was clearer than ever before and my sorrow just melted away like a snow melting in warmth of the sun shine

I felt deep current flowing in me…the love as I felt the warmth of the eyes of my wife and my children and they were waiving their hands…'Be happy daddy'

As we are just fine and doing well up here in heaven and God was witnessing it all as they spoke up. I could hear the voice of my dear Sylva

Sylva, Sylva as I started crying…

'Papa. Don't cry. No cry papa' I am doing my homework fine and don't need to worry as mom is here and God is near us. I am doing just fine papa…

And my beloved Natasha was in tears…

Honey Indeed we are missing you…and the warmth of her smiles that I have not seen for years had come true as I hug her without letting her go

The clock was ticking as God has assigned time for everything it seems. Goodness God sent a stream of light to pick them up. Back home. I am again left alone as I cried deep out of my heart

God appeared to me once again and said

'Man…you seem to be talking things very serious; Just drop the body and be eternal. I will be with you ever if you have the heart filled in love'

It was like words of Christ and a deep current of love healing me, my body mind and spirit. Just let it go as Time is a continuum and help others by taking this message…

1"Time is a continuum"

God – You are Internal! How would I get over my worries? Just remember you are eternal too

Is it so?

Yes. Indeed. You are eternal if you can understand time as a continuum

 # 2 – "You are eternal"

As the message was reverberating in myself "Time is a continuum" as I recalled my past as visions of past. It did look real though, but in time it just had passed away like a movie and God kept messaging me that I am truly eternal. Remain a witness as I will be with you forever. Your family is in heaven with me, so create a heaven around you and help others

It was like a prophet, a Christ indicating a message to me as I woke up next morning as I looked very young, at least a ten years younger

As he signed and grinned for a cup of coffee...

S.K.G: Mr. Thompson, I could see your eyes sparkling like a bright sun shine as he looked at his eyes a little closely…

Ok, now you have heard couple of messages. What are you up to...?

Indeed. I pass on the message to you my dear friend

Is it so? Am I qualified to receive the message of an incredible messiah!

Ah! If I am Incredible, so you are! As much as I carry the wealth of consciousness; you do have it in yourself as he signed at my heart. Patting on my shoulders

Sen, My young man...where are you from?

mmm...I am from India!

well done. The land I'd call it as the spiritual host!

What would you do if earth is under attack by the aliens from space?

Of course I'd protect myself, family, and then whatever is possible to save the world.

'This is exactly what I was expecting Sen...'

'Well. The alien is not in the space, within us in the community which you will need to fight against. You will be discouraged in several steps as you would need to be courageous, brave and come what may as you would think'

 'Do not stop. Until I hear the last child on earth stops crying'

Yes. Of course. Take this message with you and start at the grass root levels. Indeed you need the consciousness to grow, but without the physical well-being, mental well-being isn't possible

*

My Last day at Work, Troy, Michigan, United States

The words were haunting me…am I qualified to receive the message and how I can ever build up something in people as we have too many organizations of spiritual context. How can I spread cross the message of Mr. Thompson!!!

S.K.G.…we have a project deadline as I was back to my desk on an upcoming Project with Ford. We have won a proposal few months ago with the first milestone was pending…

Well. Here is the plan as I discussed with the team with a challenge to deliver the project. I worked in Troy, MI in a software consulting firm; I drove early in the morning to work to start ahead of rest of all to remain abreast of the client requests.

After six months of efforts with over sixteen hours a day including the weekends.my boss called me

Your team has done it very well... Congrats and I am going to forward your name for the award

Thanks Chendil. I'd rather request you for a team award.

That's the spirit young man …as he walked the talk to award the team in few weeks.

The entire team was jubilant with the songs, and partying the whole week as I remained calm to make an announcement

Friends, I have an important announcement. I mean. Today is my last day at work. What? As the team asked in chorus. Yes. I am moving back to India, Trichy my hometown

I've missed a lot in these five years of my work though I enjoyed every moment of my work in the US. I would like to thank this Nation for providing opportunities to excel and spot the right talent, and nurture them. However, my thought is not to settle for some wealth, as I derive deepest satisfaction with a responsibilities in taking back with the message s of Mr. Thompson...helping the poor. I would like to start with my Country, and extend beyond the shores of Africa where Mr. Thompson is originally from

I have found my roots of consciousness; just want to hold on to it and sail where it takes me.

The atmosphere changed as each one of us, including myself was speechless. As I asked. .but Sen... You could do it from here, US right?

Jay. No it is not possible as I have to start at the grass roots of Governance. A lot more to do and monitor inch by inch every possible workout that I have to. And the leadership skills that I have developed in recent times, Technology that I have learnt' is all required for me to support the poor and young children to being with…

Ok. I appreciate your step forward and we wish you all success in your endeavors and we promise to support you in the challenges ahead and road map was not easy

I spent almost six months in blueprint at the grass root level with finally shortlisted Thenur village for resolving the conflict that I've observed over months. I just educated them…

'Yempa.why do you fight with each other. They are all your brothers regardless of caste and creed or Religion. Did you know you are all made of the same stuff?'

'Ahda poonga sir…we are fighting because we get paid for the clashes at times and fed a plat meal and wild rum'

I was shocked to hear that and based on my enquiry found there have been number of political wings rooted in the clashes for no reasons at all.

I ran from the pillar to the pole for the NGO setup with the lack of basic infrastructure. First I decided to build a home for myself and a few poor people. At least ten homes to support the impoverished. I looked at the bricks making and studied a simple and profound technique to make bricks, as we did brick by brick with some masonry to build a nice home

I had architected the homes for each of the family. A simple home which is neat and clean with enough space for a family. By the time, collector has approved my orders. Needless to state the relentless walks and cycling to the collector office to demonstrate the pitiable living conditions of the community

I show cased one of the children who died in diarrhea and another one who was malnourished with relevant facts of at least ten families whom I had surveyed in less than couple of months. With the support of my friends, and my capital was good enough to start the constructions

After day and night of couple of months, my home was ready…as I walked in with a determination to build a hospital with the image of 'Vijaya' reminding me several times about the venture. I asked collector for the approval at the center of the village 'Thenur', at the North East where most of them work and live. To make it affordable in terms of facilities and commute. Often time's success comes in after arduous journey through the Sahara deserts; when SKG was looking for funds after the initial setup it was very hard with the Organic farming not yielding the produce and the agriculture was down due to the extreme draught conditions…there was no good news

Uncle. Uncle .as the girl child Sheila was crying for his attention. Uncle is busy. Tell me as he tried to avoid her….embedded deep in his laptop! Uncle. I have passed in I std in rank # 1.as her eyes gleamed and her mother dedicated SKG's support in his endeavor

"Sami...Yenga pollanga padikanumnoo padupadareenga...Neenga nalla erukonum...vunga vamsam nalla erukkomnum. Neenga 100 year's vazhanum ayya" with her tears foaming in her eyes;

"Sir. It is because of your efforts that our children who are impoverished are able to study well. And you are determined to make each of them an Engineer, Doctor as a learned men and women. I wish you live over hundred years, and your family to live in prosperity. May God wish you all good health? Prosperity and happiness"

As I stood speechless witnessing the sequence of events in his study room. In that moment, I realized my entire career of just working for money and passion for projects faded a million miles away and all my success have gone deep under rubble. Isn't this Love and sacrifices and the joy that I felt in the current of love was astounding and it touched my heart as well.

SKG...in a simple attire of dhoti and a cotton shirt. Amma. I just did my duty

And the humbleness and grace in his eyes were multiplying every day as he was not getting in to the political debate in any of the occasions that I have witnessed as his approach was like Swami

Vivekananda…and the student loves him a lot for his ardent skills in teaching computers to the children

Inga parungal Uncle as someone interrupted me by saying…Enjarunga 'paint brush la painting panniten' She was smiling, seeing her digital prints of Kodak moments of wisdom…As I was touched by the angels of wisdom wanting to tell me something and the under current flow in my heart was astounding and each day passed by with sequences of life transforming events as I started enjoying the small hut, a sumptuous lunch and a modest dinner in Rhagi roti and the early morning porridge with children around me, brought in memories of my past childhood.

 I could see my search for happiness in each of these eyes of children, and the smiles of men and women as they enjoyed the harvest festival of 'Sankaranti' as a token of appreciation of cattle, labors and the Sun GOD who has helped in a good harvest. SKG was there with the pot filled in rice from the farm and he lighted after praying something to the SUN GOD. When I enquired he said….'I am saying thank God for another morning with your grace filling my inner self with courage to continue till the extent possible'

And the ladies started singing, with children dancing everywhere. And the old men and women were busy preparing side dishes to serve the rest of the people around there. The plantain leaves were ready to serve. It was a good lunch with sweet pongal (made of steam rice and jaggery). Indeed the best meal that I have ever had in my life with simple pongal, and vada a spicy doughnut made of urid dhal. It was delicious and the crowd left with few children watching television and someone busy enquiring about the homework for the day!

Do you ever sleep? as I asked SKG…with a little smile. Jay, If I sleep, who would take care of these children as he sighed teaching basic grammar to a child in the Ist grade. 'Past – Presence and Future tenses....'Did you get it? As she nodded her head busy preparing for upcoming tests conducted in the school…

Anna, Anna talk to my friend who is addicted to alcohol…he walks in, with the student cum addicted host. And asks him the reason, first he never said no to it. He was rather confronting the situation to identify the real self in the person, almost after an hour of counseling, the person seem to have agreed to get over his addictions. SKG offered him to work in his farm for next 30 days and the prescription of an alternate sweet curd prepared for him every morning.

I rang up the adolescent kid after couple of months to find his scores have improved and his parents were thanking SKG for his support in counseling the child. Sir. As Mari said with tears rolling down. I feel happy now, since you listened to me and my weaknesses patiently offered me help for no reason at all and I was touched by your love. Which was like a mother advising her child? I will be there for you till my life time saar in every step you take. Mari is a strong buy with a circle of influence in his terms. Who kept weeping for a while…

"Azhathada thambi…just look at me. I am your brother. we should help each other da"

"Thambi vudayan padaikoo anjan"

"The one who has brother is not afraid of any wars" As he washed his tears away…just go-ahead with your duty and continue with your studies and work in the field. I need your support in the organic field…

Ok thalaiva. I will be there for you at any time as he whispered in his ears and started walking in his folded lungi and Hawaii chap pal calling SKG as the savior 'Yenga Vooru Kavakaroo'.

Sunday, October 3, 2010

I raised these quest within myself early in the morning just preparing myself to do the farming…before the sun rise even before the cock woke up. I stood still with my open arms looking at the distant planets….aren't we supposed to be as happy as they are in the twinkling stars?

Many of these days, I keep questioning myself what I would do if I decide to just be an individual person of help to those who are suffering. I would be able to relate my emotions more truly without the constraints of being part of an organization. I would truly be a nomad moving from one place to another doing whatever little help, making those small differences, adding life skills and passing on my values.

Perhaps, I would have no one to command but just be a partner for someone, some groups of human beings who want solace in life and a better tomorrow. I would just be answerable to my own conscience and to those lives I am part of. There will still be goals, changes, improvements, setbacks but no reports to write about, nothing to tell anyone.

Deep inside, this is me..these are the reasons Payir was founded. My life is meant to be lived this way. Now, it hurts with such pain that no longer my life is this way.

Why is it, people have to find a motive with Payir except other than these? While I understand and value discussions, debates and sharing ideas, Why is it, people want to push their own "development theories and timelines" when I live my life only for these ideals? Why is it sometimes, "the purpose and effect of use" of donations/contributions not only be explained but rationally proved?! Why it, Payir and I is are not considered as an instrument in and for the community and every minute of our existence goes on thinking about the community we share our lives with?

My journey continues in search of a better answer than the narrow constraints of being part of an organization ... knowing and working with its own practical limitation.

Core Principles of Payir

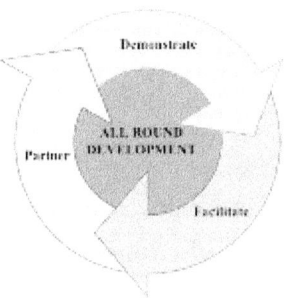

The principles of rural empowering reverberating in my veins., as a I am drawing courage from the cosmos, with my desires to light every child in the world

We inaugurated the Thenur Village Hospital on 30th Nov, 2008. The District collector of Perambalur, Shri. Anil Meshram IAS, presided over the function

PAYIR was born on the January 24th 2005 with a broad banner stating:

'PAYIR RURAL EMPOWERMENT FOUNDATION'

Thenur is a typical caste-based village in Tamil Nadu where agriculture is the most important occupation. It is situated in the newly created Perambalur district carved out from the Trichy district. As it is, Thenur lies on the southern border of these two districts which in turn poses its own set of administrative challenges? Some of the administrative departments come under the jurisdiction of Perambalur and some

Other with Trichy.

Thenur has a population of about 3500 belonging to some 13 different castes and at least 2 different religions –Hindu and Islam, predominantly the former. There is a clear area demarcation for the Schedule Caste and the Schedule Tribe community. Going by the panchayat records, about 50% of the 550+ households fall under the marginal income group while at least 50 families fall below the poverty line. About 25% of the households are landless laborers – most of them either surviving on landed agriculture/live-stock farms or dependent occupations and others work as stone breakers, well diggers, construction workers on daily wage scale. Some youths have started migrating to the city as shop-workers or as temp workers in knit industries. Thenur has quite a vibrant milk society contributing significantly to the local economy. Thenur has a middle school till Standard 8th, otherwise, it lacks in most of the community infrastructure.

Thenur' s children and youth community largely reflect current Indian statistics – they form about 60 – 70 % percent of the population but with their resourcefulness not tapped properly. The school dropout rate at middle school is more than 80%. The reason to detail the above aspects is Tamil Nadu, India because facilitating development and growth of this resource pool may turn out to be Payir's main area of work at Thenur –providing a value based education covering different age-groups and needs, creating alternate and interesting job opportunities within the village community, facilitating rural entrepreneurs, facilitating need based and balanced infrastructure development could be our engine while rural health, rural sanitation could just be a kick start.

On March 10th, Payir's formal initiation into the village community happened. During a dual purpose meeting to discuss on the temple kumbakishesham (consecration) and Payir, the Chairman of the Trust and the headman of this meeting introduced the Payir team to the village elders. The village elders group constituted of at least a couple of representatives from each of the different communities, but for the lower caste who are normally not consulted in this type of decision making or meeting.

My Challenges

The evolution of Payir had indeed took me several relentless nights from drawing the blueprint for success on the board, discussing in village Panchayat to discussions with officials. The Payir team detailed to the gathering the plans for the village and solicited their help and support in all phases and aspects of the project, and in cases where our approach may contradict current practices requested their involvement, patience and understanding during those times. We had a couple of rejuvenating experiences from the meeting. Immediately after hearing the site location for the hospital and our challenge to get an easier access point to the facilities, a number of villagers came forward to discuss with the land owner adjacent to whose land the proposed approach road lies. Not just stopping there, they were so enthusiastic to dream up an entrance arch work be fitting the facility.

SKG…'Sir..we need have identified a larger site adjacent to your site for the village empowerment office'

Veluchamy 'I do not care'

It is hard to crack the nuts as I thought after a heated argument between the villagers and the land owner…

This is my land and I will not sell it to anyone…and he left

At times Nature wants us to wait, perhaps indefinetly as the project was delayed without being able to procure this land which was right in the middle of the proposed plan for the Payir office, hospital and school.

'Oh my God…' as I gasped with my open arms facing the skies. If at all, I could fly..would go to heaven's to yell at God who has created us!

 A few months later…Veluchamy came forward

'Thambi…Neenga yennudaya landa eduthukonga' take my land

I was calculating a price in my mind. How much as I asked
'Thambi..oru paisa venam'

I didn't know the reason as I went back. Perhaps God would have heard my prayers…as I thanked him

After a week later Preeti indicated it me

"Avunga ponnu 'Rajamani' is suffering from Tuberclosis….who….." (his daughter is suffering from TB)

Who is that girl who ?

Do you remember the lean girl who was approaching us for an emergency medication, admitted at our temporary van

Oh my God. Of course I do remember

She is the one…OMG

What a game that Nature has played as I thought….all is set and move on to the required

Team – Get start go. Now find the ways to procure required materials for construction

Here is the blueprint. I will consult an Engineer to form the layout.

Ok Sir

The team after completing the morning breakfast of kepankoozh (porridge) and a banana with the strength of thousand elephants, they marched along with the master following his trails of wisdom

Here is the proposed homes for ten of them..my home in the center. No power is required for me, as I will manage, ensure we have the French window here…and the arch and the open window to discuss with the public. A greeting hall to meet the village leaders. Etc.

There was no prayer hall. Sir ?

My entire house is a prayer hall, and my villagers are the messangers of God as he walked away looking at the 10 bed hospital plan

Here is the emergency ward…by the time in dusk he moved back to the temporary abode. With a few still discussing his plans!

After a light supper…of a cup of rice, dhal and roti..he dosed off!

What an incredible messenger as I witnessed him working dawn to dusk, as I moved back in project work just thinking as a futile efforts to managing the project work, which was not getting anywhere!

At the sidelines of the meeting, a gentleman hailing from the village but running a garment factory in the city, suggested that he could make use of our rural entrepreneur programme. by sending value addition work like embroidery and knit-work to the village.

While the support and enthusiasm shown by the villagers to the project is a major thrust force, it is a blessing that the village panchayat president (elected village council head) is a graduated youngster. We instantly struck a rapport and are on our way to building a strong friendship.

Mr. Sethuratnam and his family formally donated their ancestral farm at Thenur (close to 7 acres) to the Trust on March 11th. Mr. SKG's first taste of the working of Government Revenue department happened during this land registration process. In preparation for the registration, he had met the Sub-Registrar a few times trying and finally being able to explain to him the nature of the project and our value system. He thought he had equally impressed on the document writer, whose office acts as a private support mechanism to write and furnish the necessary documents, and was convinced that the process would go in a straight forward manner. The registration process also went smoothly and coming out of the office, the Payir team was quite happy that all the patient waiting in the office (almost 5 days over a few weeks) substituted the regular bribe method
.

Next, going to the document writer's office to pay the fees, the team was shocked to learn that his charges included the bribes for the Sub-Registrar - an understanding worked out by that officer to evade anticorruption raids. The team tried to make sense with the office and could have fought till the end, but decided not to, considering that Mr. Sethuratnam, a senior citizen who is already dejected with the wane of the system, would have been pulled through the entire accompanying muddle.

After this experience and over the past few months, we have tried to plan a little better and be much clearer on our attitude to bribe at the start itself. Even then, we had been pushed to pay bribes in certain cases - all of them as last minute surprises. The first major challenge at the village turned out to be a beautiful experience, confirming our belief in the existence of well-developed village civic system. The proposed path from the main road to the project site runs on the banks of the public storm drain. Normally in the village, the land owner, in this case our farm's neighbor – a resident of Sri Lanka, adjacent to such public lands claims ascertain area of the bund as an acceptable encroachment by way of maintaining the drain. Although we had the council's as well the majority of the village people's consent to lay the path, we decided to also have the neighbor's favorable consent.

The Payir team approached the neighbor through his daughter in India as well by way of phone and mail to him. To this, he summarily rejected any proposal to lay a road besides his land. We later approached the village people for a decision and they came with this master plan. The villagers decided to first send some of the neighbor's relatives and people from his caste/community to negotiate on a settlement. If this did not turn favorable, village elders from the different communities along with the village president and the Payir team will meet the neighbor while he is in India. If necessary, the final salvo will be a village meet authorizing the path way and the neighbor's own community's commitment to standby the decision in case the neighbor decided to take legal course.

Going by the first plan, we came to know that the neighbor was in actual expecting a settlement money about 10 times the prevailing worth of such area required for the path way!! To this, the Payir team made it very clear on their side of negotiation, which was 75% of prevailing cost and a fence on the side of the path adjacent to the neighbor's land.

Rolling out the second plan, the village representatives and SKG, representing Payir, choreographed their negotiating position before the meeting. Mr. Senthil was asked to sit tight during the entire meet while the villagers did the talking!! During this pre-meeting, to a complete surprise, the villagers came with a master-stroke – that the neighbor's community will bear the entire settlement cost if in case the neighbor was insistent on money. The only say the Payir team had during the meeting was that the neighbor should either give his consent free of cost as his part to the whole effort or our settlement cost was non-negotiable. The choreographing was so perfect that during the actual meeting the neighbor's conscience was completely kindled and he could take no other position than to settle the issue free of cost with a happy mind!

He even took us out for a dinner and has lately been very interested and supportive in our works!
Thenur is a dry land area dependent entirely on rains for water. The past few years of drought and incessant drilling of bore and tube wells has meant that the water table has gone well below 200 feet in many places. The current well in the farm has only sufficient water to irrigate about 60% of the farm. So, we decided to drill a bore after due geological testing. Even after drilling 260 ft., the bore did not yield water which meant a good amount of money down the drain. By June end, the well had just 5 ft. water.

We had also started the foundation digging activity of the hospital blocks and were quite concerned on proceeding further on the construction activity. While we were able to locate another source of water point with the help of local water diviners (after the first try, the teams belief on the geological surveyors waned because we felt they did not have scientifically advanced equipment's while the success of local diviners were quite dependable at much less cost), pumping of water necessitated a separate electrical connection as the current connection was specifically for agriculture. Many had cautioned that the immediate biggest bureaucratic hurdle would be with the electricity department. Not surprisingly, they decided to go by books and apply the highest tariff slab under commercial construction which meant a minimum slab of Rs. 3000 per month for 2 KW supply and a setup cost close to Rs.20000.

In the interim the architectural design and plan were done with the help of volunteer civil engineers and architects. Architectural design reflects rural life - is simple but practical and appealing.

Most material used in the construction is low cost and environment friendly like earthen bricks, earthen tiles and thatching. Most of material for construction was locally sourced - An all-women's unit took up the brick making, using hand press machines, during course of construction.

Most of the labor for the construction came from the village. Has helped establish trust among the villagers about the mission of Payir and role they can play in their own development

The construction of reading room too has been successfully completed along similar lines to the health center. The major objective of the reading room is to provide an informal education to children of the village (4 - 14) yrs. Emphasis is on imparting useful real life education which the children can relate to and put to quick use. For the children between 4 -9 yrs. the main subjects would be Tamil and mathematics. In addition to the above the room will also serve a small library - providing newspapers, magazines and books.

A week after meeting the officials, Thenur experienced such a rainfall not seen in the past 10 years. All the storage tanks overflowed and our own farm was under a foot of water. In less than a week the farm well rose by 25 feet!

Along with this, the dug foundations caved in. Even though this meant re-work, all worries for water were also washed away for the entire year. With more rains on the forecast, Payir team decided to push at a faster pace the foundation work even if it meant jumping the law by using the existing agricultural water source for construction activity. We do not have an easy solution with respect to electrical power, unless we decide to give into the officials which would mean a substantial recurring expense. With our current setup, there is likelihood that the officials will harass the team by sending audit squads, but we have decided to take it head-on.

This To "power" overcome challenge, the Payir team has made a conscious decision to harness the Solar power for our entire electrification. A project proposal is on the works and will be sent to you in a week's time for your perusal. Our working team has been growing in the past few months as the construction activity is getting heated up. Kathir Anna, an accomplished civil engineer and a real estate developer at Trichy, is our project and site engineer, Pudhuma who has crafted a beautiful work with the site architecture (she left to US this week to do her Masters) and Valli akka, our Trust's financial auditor and adviser – we were looking for a very honest person here and could not have asked for any one better, these 3 provide the directions to the grass-root team. Our grass-root team has Priya, a Gandhi gram product, taking multitude of supervisory role covering people, time, inventory, farm and accounts; 3 skilled masons on sustainable and cost effective building - Karuppiah from Gandhi gram, Balu and Maran from Gudalur; Selvakumar, a local, mobilizes and supervises the local work force which now numbers close to 20; Marudhai Annan – Selva's father who has been cultivating the farm for decades is the eyes and ears for all local knowledge.

We also have an expert advisory team which consists of Dr. Yogananda of Mrinmayee on all structural engineering aspects; Dr. Sridharan and Dr. Srihari – our own doctors and Mr. Suresh Babu on financial and auditing matters. We are getting tremendous advisory support from Gi and Tha - the good doctors of Sittilingi (www.tribalhealth.org), Founders of Thulir (www.thulir.org) - Anu and Krishna who are also architects and Dr. Karunakaran – VC of Gand higram University.

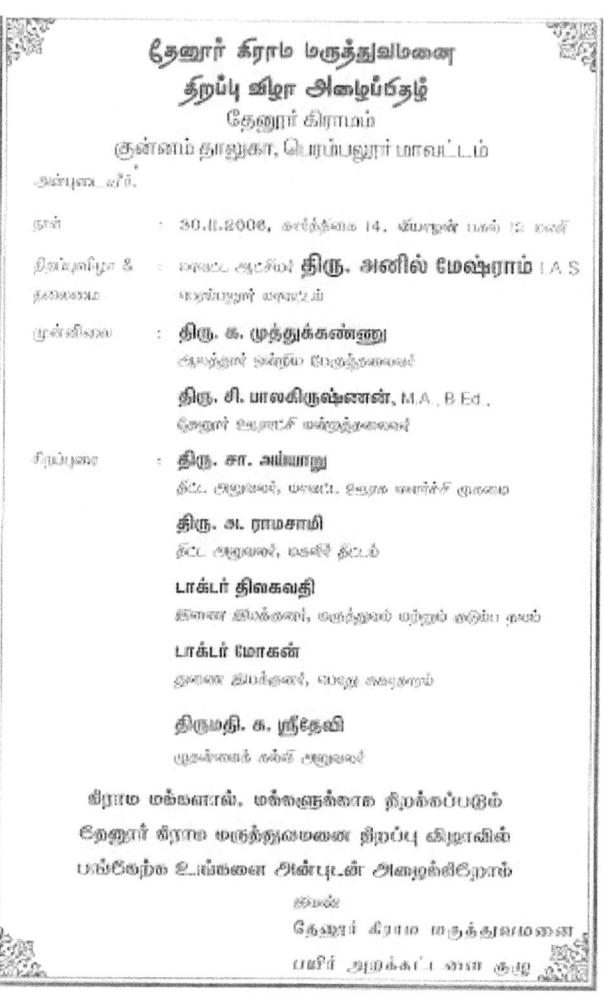

An invitation printed in the local language inviting on
the inauguration of the thenur village hospitals

Rural Empowerment Facilitation center

The basic belief that every human being deserves a good quality of life is the purpose of the Rural Empowerment Facilitation center. Quality of life is, of course, relative. For an Indian village, good quality of life means unhindered access to primary health care, primary and middle level education, a sustained income that meets every day needs, and a satisfactory family, social and spiritual life.

The mission of Payir is to facilitate in the transformation of Indian villages into socially stimulating, self-sustaining, growth-oriented communities. We believe that to achieve this transformation it is necessary to have a holistic approach, where all aspects of challenges in rural life are addressed.

1. Education for all
2. Job skill development program
3. Organic Farming &
4. Efforts to source electricity through solar power
5. Self Help groups (with de-addiction planning centers for counseling)
6. Health Care centers, Schools
7. Empowering Panchayat Governance
8. Implementing best practices in Agriculture

Chapter 3 TRANSFORMING INDIVIDUALS

The number of volunteers, branches, Friends of Payir (FoP) is ever increasing, and the network of wellwishers worldwide is overall a lakh from every corner of the world and the number is ever increased year over year.

'Left, Right. March...as S.K.G, the leader of contemporary India was leading the march past. With the ardent leadership of an IT giant who is in simple attire of Gandhian dhoti was walking along his way leading thousands of children with the morning prayer. With the network of several all NGO's following his footpath in transforming villages, and the social media is extending SKG's vision beyond shores from South Arcot to SFO.

Each of these children are taught to meditate, practice simple techniques of breathing to form a community of mental and physical strength. Each of these children would become a Scientist, Teacher, Professor, Social Activist, Engineer, Doctor, and Artist. Above all, they would also transform as an Individual and a good human in evolving consciousness. They would expand the vision of Payir to the world across boundaries with no barriers or anything whatsoever, where the consciousness is where the Payir team would belong, and not restricted by the man-made boundaries or layers of mind.

Jay 'I will be there in a minute; training few students for the upcoming Independence day celebrations

My Childhood
When I was studying in Sathanur village, there were few instances that I had witnessed. It is in my conscious mind as the cry of the mother is still there deeper in my heart!

"Early in the morning as the cock cooing 'cockaracoo…as it is little perturbed for some reason. My grand-mom takes care of pregnant women, as in those days there were very few hospitals. My village was not an exception, as we need to go to a hospital almost 30-40 kms away from the village by crossing the local village roads which takes hours to pass by

"Is someone there…Vijaya ma is suffering from extreme pain. Can you help her?"

My grand mom woke immediately, and started walking towards the balcony to sigh that she will be there in a minute.

She was there and there was a complication in the childbirth as the mother was crying louder for help. My grand mom had arranged for the bullock cart to support to take her to the nearby hospital

Vijaya. Just stay calm. We will take you to the nearest hospital in town. Just hang in there…as she kept talking to her to keep her conscious to avoid any further complications

About 10 kms downs the trail, wheel of the bullock cart fell into a pit, and it was difficult to raise the wheels. Mari who was riding the cart had to jump as he tried to life the wheels, which didn't help and called for help…

"Anyone there" please help us as he frantically cried for help. Where there wasn't anyone

"Bah bah ……go. Get the hell out of here" as he kicked the bulls to try…finally, after his arduous attempt for half an hour, he was able to get it back on track and the bullock cart started moving at a reasonable speed..By now, Vijaya was almost fainting. Vijaya, Vijaya listen to me as my grand-mom kept sprinkling water in her face to keep her awake!

Finally it took almost couple of hours reaching the hospital in town, didn't realize that there would other challenges.

My grandmother and Mari carried Vijaya ma in to the emergency ward…and there was none in the hospital with a security who was dosed off…

Hello, hello, here is an emergency please call the duty doctor to help!!! Vijaya is pregnant, and she will need immediate help.

Uh…uh.as the security woke up and he said

'Amma…these duty doctors sometime they come, but mostly they are busy in visiting hospitals in town and cities as they pay them well'

Oh my God. We are paying for the Doctors as we form the Governments as Mary yelled at the security.

'Hold on. I will call the chief'

'Dr. There is a patient who is in emergency' Can you come here soon..?

Velu. I live here in town, and it will take at least 1 hour to reach up there. Ask the Nurse to administer emergency care"

As Venu hang up the phone….Vijaya was unconscious.

Amma. Vijaya...please look...look...you will be fine.

The chief Nurse administers some medications after checking her pulse rate. The pulse rate is dropping...let me take her to the emergency ward.

This could be a syserian case which I cannot help... need the chief to be here.

After a while the Chief arrives. And there was no pulse rate at all. Dr. Dr what happened

'She is dead' I am sorry. It was just another patient for the Chief. The only mother of a two children is dead for lack of medical help on-time.

The next morning was a Panchayat lead who claimed so many reasons of the lack of responsiveness so on and so forth as it happens every year as part of the regular panchayat meetings. My father and I were there in the meetings, as a kid I raised a question:

'Sir. Why did you kill the mother?'

Damn it. What did you say? I did not kill anyone. My dad is a modest person, who did not want me in troubles, as he said. S.K.G. Just be quiet. We cannot change the world.

'No papa. I will change my surroundings as much as possible'

The above incident was deeply rooted in my conscious and I was looking for answers within during my high school talking to my friends about the basic needs of humans:

Though I was a carefree boy, I did well in studies and asked questions to my friends and teachers who had answers to most of it.

In my history class:

"Sir. It is great to heart the glory of India in the past. How can we regain in the future?

Well. Good question. The reason is a good governance practices in those days with ministers and local administrators for every 1000 people and the visits of the king helped in taking care of individuals"

I thought about this…and the death of Vijaya which was haunting me, even in my dreams. In that night, I had a dream where Vijaya was crying for help…

'Appo, Nee thangachiya paathu kiviya paa'

Meaning, would you take care of my younger daughter please?
As my tears started rolling down…and my mom asked me. What happened S.K.G?

Mom. Nothing I am fine.

Just sleep well da. There is nothing we could do!

As I continued with my studies and busy in exams as usual with the cricket was my passion of those days.

First was born a hospital, with a doctor in attendance every day and specialists from Tiruchi visiting once a month. The next was a non-formal learning center, which incorporates traditional knowledge in farming and watershed management and weaving in its curriculum while meeting the minimum level of learning prescribed by NCERT. A data entry center, which gives exposure to rural youth to computers, while providing them a source of income has also been opened in a seven-acre extent of land donated by S.K.G' s uncle Sethuraman. With some difficulty, he has obtained broadband facility for the center.

"When I looked at the transformation of villages in last two to three decades in Thenur, and many more villages. There were no major changes, as I have noticed"

He dreamt about it since his school days to work for a decade to fulfill his personal financial commitments before venturing in to the social activities

It was not easy in the beginning after returning from the US. There was a phase of close to a year with several questions from the localities with a raise bro's of whether Payir would sustain, or perhaps Payir has the ability to transform

The financial commitment is huge; I had been using all the finances that I earned from the US for the initial hospital. I request each of you to donate denominations of Rs.100/ to support each of these children,

Like a flow of river and the message of a Mahatma with his unique views. Perhaps if you realize the sufferings around, you must create an impact to visualize. There is a lot that you can teach by expending two hours a month, or a business plant and many things in small steps for instance a Doctor who can help part time

"Arise, Awake and STOPNOT Till the Goal is reached"

- Swami Vivekananda

I was about fifteen years when I was studying in High School in Trichy…It happened

'Dear Students, hurry up, we have called your parents. Our school will remain shut for next couple of days due to an emergency. You all can go home now…' as my class teacher who always takes care of notes and the timeline was in a hurry to go back home, followed by a short announcement from the Headmaster. Reverad.Father. Tambaku. Students there is a serious problem outside, stay together as we would drop each of you back home

In the Gandhi road, there were barricades and Police force with gunmen and watershed and teargas to find some men carrying weapons were arrested…as I pass through the street, a trajectory of stone hit my forehead…perhaps it looked like a perfect situation…

Amma, amma as I felt through the pain and I started crying. The care take, Mohan had immediately held with his handkerchief and asked me to be seated

I didn't know what happened for almost 45 mins there were many military vehicles, and our bus was stopped for more than half an hour. What is going on ? as I asked….

There is a communal rage. If someone ask you about your caste. Say that you are a Christian!!! And tell your name as Vincent

As the advice came in from my senior…rightly said there were few men looking for more to cremate as we were haunted by the dreadful eyes and wanting to massacre people for no reason at all

The incident had left me in a state for almost a week till the life was back to normal with the loss of men, women and children mounting up to hundred as indicated in the newspaper

'Appa…anything that we can do to change that?'
'of course, you can. When you become an adult and a good politician to teach people about the results of what they are doing to their children'

'Now. It is your homework and higher education as he indicated his plans for me for the future'

Ok daddy. As I gasped through the window

My house in Trichy is a beautiful one with a back yard for cows where my maid milks the cow in the morning, a pair of pigeon that I feed in the morning. The cooing cocks are brave enough over the roof top.

My dad and I take care of the garden filled with roses, hibiscus, and some medicinal herbs that my dad had planted; especially I could remember the scent of the eucalyptus plant whenever I helped my dad in the garden

My siblings are modest without many fights when I grew up, Indeed they taught me in maths, and science to excel them in both these subjects as I exclaim.

The house is one of the ancestral properties, with the large pillars supporting the ceiling, and the central space for rain water harvesting..(muttram) as we call The hall was very spacious with 'unjal' that can host at least four to five, in those days I spent mostly in the Unjal whenever I am back from the school to my sister's envy

The traditional house had simple architecture with the basics of ample air and light circulation everywhere...as I realized the offices covered with glass and you gaze the clouds like a prisoners.

I looked back as a stranger with the build modest huts which are really comfortable than the contemporary brick and mortar houses as I could smell the ground and the warmth of the bamboo pillars around. It was simple to withstand rain, and sun. With required window panels of large French architect with glasses designed by children, the so called impoverished fingers have painted beautiful pictures of what they felt and loved in hills, and rivers. My home for next couple of days was well lit with an oil lamp was just amazing with no pollution to the environment. Which itself is a social service in my view...and the poor children were around playing happily and the master arrives...S.K.G there was a pin drop silence, as they love him so much and let him talk

I exclaimed within myself. How may I wonder a thousand families are dependent with over five years of day/and night of SKG efforts are just imminent. It portrays a beautiful picture of his self and image grown larger in over a thousand household. He has not done anything for any reason or gain or even without any anticipation

Each of these children calls him by 'Anna, Yenga Vooru Shivaji' The warrior of my village, and they think this man has hailed from the heavens. Now. I have become one among these children with a similar thought of this man from the heavens. Perhaps a messenger of Thenur village, and I wish him extend his wings to every part of the world where human consciousness strives hard to survive...and I wish and pray to God to give him enough wealth and power to accomplish what he is desiring for the future generations

'Pasangla. Homework panniteengala…Did you do your homework?' Yes sir. And No sir from a few back bench crew members. After completing the sessions for an hour and a half, he picked up a chat with those adolescent kids for keeping their focus.

I found SKG was rejoicing with children and the reason for some smiles…with the songs of Bharathiyar

'Jaathi ellaiyadi papa
Kula thaazchi vuyarchi sollal paavam'
"There is not any lower or upper caste,
My dear children….remember discriminating
Someone by caste/birth is a sin"

Thus, infusing the idealism through the young minds shaping clays in to diamonds and I am sure each of these children of the future generations would sprout as a true citizen of this country.

'Pasangla. You need to stay, three of you. Thalamuthu, Hari and Sebi follow me. He takes them to his home to teach them a simple breathing practices called 'Nadhi Suddhi' a profound technique for concentration by streamlining breathing…After a year, I hear from them..especially Thalamuthu has passed with over 80% in the 10TH GRADE was just amazing as I felt it was way beyond any expectations. Indeed SKG has won a battle by improving % passes in almost seven schools and there are many schools which are in the list of PAYIR to empower children and encourage'

When SKG was visiting the neighboring villages, he found so many Kinder Garden children were malnourished. He found one falling down in the prayer sessions out of extreme heat. He just examined and the town hospital doctor confirmed her for the malnutrition…while some of the kids in the country are obese. Here is an hundred children those who are malnourished.. Immediately the day after, the master blaster thinks about a program plan with the decisive approach to solve a problem in the resolution plane of his mind in his astute way of solving problems

Team; 'Let us build a Nutrition Plan' as he typed a few points in his laptop to build a plan for the future. Which is serving over a hundred children in various schools and number of projects is ever increasing.

Facilitated by the interaction between Payir and the local villagers a self-help group has been formed by the villagers. This group has come together to self-finance and run a small diary project. This group consists of both men and women, which is significant considering currently the village women are not part of any initiative outside their homes. Also notable is the fact that idea was conceptualized and brought to fruition by the villagers themselves, with Payir merely playing an advisory role.

Payir believes that this is a milestone in our efforts.

We hope that this fuels development of more self-groups, which would take us further in the stated objective of empowering the villagers.

Effort to source electricity through solar power:
We are in advanced stages of finalizing on a plan to generate electricity (1.5 KW) for electrifying the whole project using solar panels.

Vocational training:
We intend to provide meaningful vocational training to village youth that can be used a source of income. Some ideas are - auto repair (mainly two wheelers), motor winding.

Leadership training: One of our efforts is to develop local leadership. We hope to put together a program on basics of law, panchayat raj and general leadership skills.

*

'The inspection letter from the chief and Dr. Tom Jeyachandran (January 8th – 14th 2008) who has audited several health care centers around the world has some remarks on the progress. I did not want to settle for anything small' and the letter as I hold read this…highlighting all my challenges. I used the risk mitigation plan of back up resources based on anticipated risks as IBM had taught me the principles of managing risks…Our education is not a waste as it helped often to make right decisions.

I picked up a volunteer in Payir a young man named 'Muthu'…
J: Muthu, what do you do with the Payir organization..

M: Sir, I belong to Payir.

What do you mean?
This is my country and SKG is my mother!

Can you explain a little bit about the way you got into the Payir organization…

M: Well Buddy! I would like to know your background

It was my childhood, everything my father and my neighbors, friends and God did not intend to set it right until the day I met SKG sir.

Hold on. Indeed, God has sent you SKG?

Yes. Ok. God has finally opened his eyes

No..no…Indeed. You have opened your heart!
Ok ok.

I was convicted and sent to Jail for three months due to consuming illicit liquor, during this time my mom and sister were taken care by Payir and thanks to SKG who had counseled me . not just by asking me to be good, by showing me the way to be good through services.. I realized it when my mom was in the brink of committing suicide…

Sami (God) mare vanthu kapathitaru!!!
He Saved me and my family..I don't have words of my gratitude…as he spoke with tears rolling down.

Ok ok…well done my friend as I spoke to him…with SKG looking clearer than ever with his gleaming eyes of confidence with absolute integrity, and humbleness

*

Here is it ….despite all the hardships, the first health care center. And I am determined doing it in every single villages in India and anywhere in the world, as every human being is entitled for the basic benefits. If the respective Governments are not doing it. I will doing it for the people of the world and for every global citizen

PAYIR Health care Center:

The ardent leader has not stopped his desire of basic needs of survival. Beyond and above, he wanted each of them to work hard and be self-sustainable in the projects of BPO with 11 computers with few companies outsourcing it from Chennai. It is a small facility with a potential scope of expansion

SKG had discussed with few companies in Tirupur and trying to take another project for village people. With ten tailoring machines with trained women is an upcoming facility with projects from Thenur

The Payir self-help groups facilitate by the interaction with the local villagers a self-help group has been formed by the villagers. This group has come together to self finance and run a small diary project. This group consists of both men and women, which is significant considering currently the village women are not part of any initiative outside their homes. Also notable is the fact that idea was conceptualized and brought to fruition by the villagers themselves, with Payir merely playing an advisory role.

Organic farming:

Payir runs an organic farm within the land donated to it. The main goal of the farm is learn, develop and train villagers on new/traditional environmentally sustainable agricultural techniques. Currently we have a paddy plantation, a coconut grove and a garden of herbs. We have started producing coconut compost within the farm; this is being used to fertilize the grove and garden. We hope to shortly make this available the villagers for them to use and sell. One of the unique feature in construction was that the material used in the construction is a low cost and environment friendly like earthen bricks, earthen tiles and thatching.

Most of material for construction was locally sourced – An all-women's unit took up the brick making,

using hand press machines, during course of
construction. we visited the site and got hand first
hand operation of the machine

Most of the labor for the construction came from the
village. I have observed there is a limited electricity
power in SKG's house, primarily used for his laptop
and broadcasts, as he vehemently denies by
saying...'let every village be lighted'. There is no TV
or music system. He has very simple cot leads his
simple life along with village people and for them.

As more and more that I pondered into the Payir's
project it was like an eternal list of project to fulfill
every child's dream, and the communities on the
whole

I was astounded to find many NGO's partnering with
PAYIR realizing SKG's potential and ability to
transform any hardship in to favoring the community
through his astute intelligence and clairvoyance. Any
bureaucracy would just wither away in his very
presence and he speaks out of the heart, reminding
me of Jack Welsch.

It is all reminiscent in my mind. Whatever quality time that I had spent with SKG is really worth remembering in every second from the simplest of things to the essence of consciousness evolving. You could see that all happening in one place in the community…educating children, singing, dancing with children would melt your heart away. If you rich enjoy by sharing, if you are poor enjoy by caring..either way you will find it as a heaven on earth for all…I invite you from my heart and spirit to visit this place..a heaven on earth.

Whoever you are , and whatever you are doing….whether Engineering, Medicine or construction of the philosophies of Gandhism or Paramahamsa…Just spend some time here observing the master..you will catch it. Let it be like a virus of truth enter in to the hearts and spirits of each of you

And your life will have a deeper meaning, perhaps a real meaning of truth evolving by observing the most happening forms of events in this community

BUILD is an international organization that is currently partnered with PAYIR

Chapter 4 THE CORE PRINCIPLES OF PAYIR

In the southern part of India. A small village in Trichy with a community haunted by the dreadful clashes and affected by poverty. Nature had no interest with the extreme drought conditions further worsening the situation; with children are malnourished, and adults without jobs seeking to relocate to nearby towns

Payir was founded in January 2005 with the mandate toe empower rural India to transform itself
Into a socially stimulating, self-reliant and growth oriented community. Payir's project in Tehnur, Near Trichy, is the Organizations first attempt to exercise the idea of holistic rural development?
To which end, Payir has set up a health center, a school, and vocational and agricultural
Training programs, among other endeavors

With the vision of transforming Panchayat schools. As per the plan, I integrated all these elementary and high schools with over one thousand children with proper teachers from the neighboring schools. Some of these teachers those who are part of the Payir organization are interacting closely with the Parents in the Parent-Teachers association, there were challenges in terms facing the anticipation of parents as we are educating every household in terms of encouraging them for higher studies

As a development plan, we have educated parents in the annual meeting, I've emphasized on empowering students with proper high-school education. The entire infrastructure for the schools and education for a year was funded from my savings earned from the US.

Early our expenses for seven schools and five health care, Tele-medicine centers with panchayat development centers. The Asha foundations in the US, formed by the Indian born citizens are funding up to 3-4 lakhs for the education. The free break-fast programme and the children with disorders during the survey with required nutrition supplement include our financials.

The Governance of Payir includes multiple layers of auditing formed by the best Chartered Accountant, Meenakshi Sundaram and the books of accounts have been appreciated by the chief. Income Tax office with the transparency in every penny spent. After reviewing all the expenditure, the 80G deduction was announced for the Payir Organization, which means income spent is eligible for tax deductions. Our financial accounts are there in the

There have been several questions from the localities in the villages, perhaps criticisms which are common and I hope and believe these people would eventually understand the funding

The future plan for the Payir organization is to streamline Panchayat Governance to empower every village. The collector, MLA's are not anywhere closer to the villages, Payir's responsibility is to empower Panchayat in order to benefit every village

I feel it is extremely important to create jobs for every adult in the villages, by providing skills. As a next step, I would like to stop addictions. I fear the consequences of alcohol consumption in the villages, especially in the adolescents and adults with affecting their personal health, family and the financial burden resulting in many deaths in the society. My goal is completely plan for the eradication of controlling addictions by provides counseling.

My vision is to strive for good quality education for each of these children who should be able to work in any part of the world. I have observed many top performers in recent times with a little push and interest inculcated. As Swami Vivekananda opined..

'Education is a means to open up your consciousnesses

My real intent is to help them achieve basic needs through enough skills and basic education, and further expanding their consciousness by research and self-inquiry. Also, give it back to the community by supporting each other anywhere in the world. I am teaching these children to support humanity. It really does not matter whether it is in India or Africa…the one who is able to create smiles around by alleviating the pains of others is the one who has done the job

On the other day. I had a dream

When God was enquiring with Chitra Gupta

About the good and bad deeds. There was a man who was caught for his bad deeds and God asked

God: Mani. You are a politician. Why didn't you help others as you had the opportunity?

Mani: I was good. Until the system changed me

Well. You have excuses. Ok. Spend some time in the community center of the heaven and then transition to heaven

The other man was bewildered as he cried

'Oh my Lord. Father, pardon my sins'

My son. You are a Christian father. Why you have so many criminal case registered

It is all a plan to malign my name as the father said…then why didn't you allow me when I was there in the church

Well. Father. You were interrupting my business

Why didn't you show me to the world

Because you were interrupting my fame!!!

I order you be thrown to hell for misguiding men and women..

This is how life continues as we are misguided and tend to misguide. As much as possible, you should be ready to help others as it brings you good deeds. The more you sow good deeds, more you would reap as the cause and effects theory. It cannot be other way!!!

Your sufferings have a reason and the social setup is the cause of all poverty in the world. God created humans or perhaps it was his manifestations as Vedanta says and you are part of it. If it is so. It was due to the greedy politicians, and a few religious leaders that you have lost the faith in god and the ability to reconnect yourself to the eternal being

You have it undiscovered as Buddha says! India, my land from time immemorial has never invaded against countries, as its primary goal was reaching the peak of the consciousness through self-inquiry and reasoning. Hence, many emperors have come out of their kingdom in search of truth. Siddhartha the Buddha is an example and many more that followed his footsteps. The Epics of Hinduism teaches you virtues of personalities such as Rama, and Krishna who had been revelations or avatars of God as mythology claims to induce some good behavior in each of you

The core principles of Payir was based on Vedanta

1. Service to humanity
2. Democratize basic needs:
   a) Quality Education for children
   b) Jobs for Adults &
   c) Empowering women

The rural empowerment plan would help every village in a micro-economic model of achieving peace and propriety. There are about 700,000 villages in India. Each of it should transform in to villages of self-reliance. Payir is willing to extend by partnering with other NGO's global and local and the Government Organizations

My goal is to reach every village in India, and every country with the world changing as one Global village with one governance with the vanishing boundaries ..As I am marching towards the goal. I didn't realize that I needed a life partner as I never intended to date anyone as I have been busy working all these days..

A ray of light and love with brimming confidence touched by the spirit from the heavens as the human turned super humans turning as messiah…
"Seek thou. Shall be given to you" as I witnessed SKG's spirit growing strong and his confidence levels were sky rocketing in everything he did. The next

plan was to implement the solar panels to generate electricity in phases for at least a hundred families. After obtaining permissions from the collector, SKG worked hard on a plan with a design to implement a protype first as it need a lot of space to generate ,store and distribute electricity

Indeed there was huge place behind the cemetery as he sought collector's permission to build his own plant. After several meetings, and discussions in the collector's office. The plan was sanctioned to produce less than 10MW of power for a hundred family in a small scale...The panels were extremely large and some were damaged in the transit

The bio recycling plant is based on the cow dung and waste management to effectively segregate and regenerated pesticides for the Organic farm, which is absolutely natural and harmless to our system. I have encouraged every household to segregate wet and dry waste and dump it in the respective bins to effectively recycle what is possible and the plastic wastes and aluminum cans form the craft sessions for our children in school, and I've instructed limited use of plastics to protect Nature, to leave a planet for the generations to come.

Jai ho as I screamed over the hill top seeing the tele medicine program going live;

Payir goes Wireless

We were able to connect wirelessly to the rest of the world with the vision of APJ's technology come true.

Friday Aug, 19th 2011 was a memorable day in the diary of Payir Trust, and Payir Innovations... We connected to the world wireless using Radio Wave transmission from our nearest telephone exchange (~5km away).

This has been a long journey which started in November 2010. We were connected to the internet over wired line from Puthanampatti exchange. BSNL ran a special line for ~5Km. We used to get ~2Mbps, which was heavily shared by the many computers in our IT center, Learning center for e-Learning, and Health center for tele-medicine. This was also the main contact line for our founder, employees and volunteers to connect to the rest of the world and spread the work we do. However running a cable for ~5km, exclusively for us with not much revenue, had its own challenges - physical, natural and human interventional. As a result, we were out of internet services for many days, sometime months...

We were brain-storming on various ideas on how to

connect wirelessly. We contacted RuTag unit in IIT-M as well. We explored various ideas which were either expensive or not feasible. Finally we had a ray of hope in Mr. Kuppuswamy, an ex-employee of BSNL, now retired and settled in Bangalore. He is part of our Friends of Payir - Bangalore Chapter. He introduced us to the Chief General Manager of BSNL Mr. Mahendrakumar, who took special interest in getting wireless connection to Payir.

The initial steps happened at a lightning pace:
- BSNL 'emerging business unit' did feasibility study in Thenur and gave the go ahead signal
- BSNL Head Telecom Office approved our request to erect a wireless Radio Wave Tower in our premises
- We got in touch with Mr. Nagaraj of Vista InfoTech, who gave special attention to Payir to get tower installed and all other necessary cabling and equipment's

Then came change of personnel in BSNL, the TN elections and things were stalled. We were patient but persistent in our goal to get wireless connectivity in Thenur, and kept talking to various people in BSNL. Finally we got the approval to install the 8Mbps modem on our tower, after a lot of last mile push.

We are now happy that our time, money and efforts have paid off, and we are getting 3-4 Mbps uninterrupted internet connection for the past 2 days. We plan to utilize this for the uninterrupted continuity of our current services, and future activities. We have the provision to transmit wireless up to 21km radius, and plan to transmit and connect many other village centers to the internet, and truly make RURAL world CONNECTS TO URBAN world a reality

We would like to thank all our supporters and well-wishers who have helped us to achieve this feat. The volunteering campaign had started very well with the students from colleges visiting often, with a few intended to stay back..

Thursday, September 16, 2010
Our broad band connection is the back bone for our Software development, E-learning initiative and Tele-Medicine – each one of them making a huge difference to our efforts here. In the first place, this type of connection to a rural area beyond the normal limits, it was a tremendous effort by the local staff of BSNL.

Lately, for the past 3 months, we have been having constant issues with this connection. And I don't think the initial level of efforts is there now to try solving the issues. Normally, such issues are not one-dimensional but our working culture wants to solve that way. In this case – distance from sender tower to us is larger than normal limits.

I think, in solving issues that has a high amount of social impact, one needs to first decongest the small bottle necks. While, a larger and permanent solution could come from the "one-dimensional" issue – the high level of technicalities, economics and time for creating such solutions means insisting on it can tremendously slow social progress.

One among them is Preeti, a homeopathic doctor who is smart, intelligent and reads minds by heart. And loves to interacting with children

Preeti, a Homeopathic Doctor, even though has been with us on and off for past couple of months, was initiated into actual community work yesterday. And it turned out to be a day to remember for her. Preeti came back from the field visit saying she can't take off from her memory the tears and the eyes that beheld it! She, with a deep thought, asked me when the house for her in the village will be ready (she is now staying in the farm). I was a little perplexed .. she told, staying there she can physically help with the construction work of Amutha's home .. the beholder of those tears.

I opined that while it is a good thought, we should also look at alternate solutions for Amutha. Preeti is just going through exactly the battles I went through when I started living with the community here. Our breed of people bleeds with the heart which actually does. For many of the policy makers, growth model managers and students of development theories Preethi's decision may seem emotional, a solution that is neither scalable nor sustainable, that has little direction and has limited impact.

On the contrary, I believe, what she is carrying now is something that will in certainty bring in happiness to the immediate life of Amutha and her son. There is an indirect consequence that this happiness spreads. That's a far better impact than many of the theories which never sees the daylight and when it does brings no solace for people like mutha. Contradictorily these policies landed her in trouble in the first place!

As I was discussing with Preeti about Amutha, the MSN page I was browsing had an article "Anil XYZ's's $1 billion home still not in the list of Forbes most expensive homes"... Jai Ho!!! I pray, Preethi's heart and her breed of people swell large enough to be some day listed in the annals of history!
Now, let me get to the day of Preethi's! She visited a few homes where our health workers found it very hard to make an impact even though care is absolutely necessary. Later she had a meeting with a group of ladies.

When coming back, she visited Amutha whose husband moved out of her life immediately after a boy was born. Amutha has very few relatives and her son is also not a healthy boy. While she goes out to do daily labor work, she is not the "strong" ones whom a farm owner/employer prefers...she can't be a load (wo)man, masons won't prefer her or she can't do paddy thrashing. She won't get work all days because of this and she may not be equally paid like the rest. Now, through a Government housing scheme she was offered a "pucca concrete" house for her thatched home.

The Government pays Rs.70,000, part of it by supplies. Like many of the ill planned schemes, some 3 lakh homes were to come in the 1st year across the state. The timing was wrong, demand shot up, prices of raw materials went up by nearly 200%. A brick which was costing Rs. 2.75 a month before is now Rs.6 .. and if the person is lucky to get a hand on it. Anyway, lot of her neighbors convinced Amutha to go for it. Now, she is caught between the devil and the deep blue sea, with her house raced down and not knowing how to finish this building!

Amutha found a patient ear in Preeti to tell all her life sorrows and sufferings. She being pushed into a dependent life all through her life and the daily suffering she has to go through, any Tom, Dick and Harry has an idea for her. I have seen many times she takes a decision which hurts her later. We can endlessly debate on the attitude change that change makers have to bring in her...but for someone who suffers day in and day out.. who is loved by very few, who goes empty stomach many days, on whom the society slants its concocted eye ... the only comfort given is love and sharing.

Monday, August 9, 2010. Do the farms look green?
How can one ever expect a man chasing greedy goals to understand what it means for a farmer when the rains disappoint him yet again? Or how it shatters a villager to see arable lands without cultivation? How can one expect a man who spends half his life in an AC chamber to understand what if feels like to stand on a parched land feeling the sun's fury on one's head

and to look into a well that shows no traces of water despite the numerous bores that scar it?

How can one ever get a man, skipping a job that pays him in lakhs for another that pays him a few thousands more, to understand how folks in the village work on all the days of the week for much longer hours and do far more strenuous work for an annual income that amounts only to those few thousands?

I believe cultivation is tough job. Constant and persistent vigilance, sheer hard work, endless perseverance is what it takes to get a good yield. In the end their crop is sold at a mere amount. So, what lies ahead for the farmers there if they don't move out and the current state of affairs don't improve? Can we hold them responsible for wanting a better standard of life that their endless efforts in their farms don't seem to accommodate? What destiny awaits these fertile lands when each farmer decides to move into towns in pursuit of better pay and a better quality of life? How do we propose to feed the huge population if such a thing ever happens?

Folks in the villages seem quite ignorant of how life in the towns is. But their ignorance seems much lesser than the ignorance town folks have about village life.

People in the cities have no clue how a village functions, and how dramatically their way of life is changing the rural life. Media seems to be barely reaching out to addressing certain issues they must have addressed ages ago. Issues that deserve all the attention they can afford to get; issues that would certainly hold much more relevance to the Indian masses than certain other news pieces that cram our media like which business tycoon is dating which actress. Misplaced priorities and misplaced focus are commonplace problems. Sometimes they don't make much difference. At other times, they make all the difference there is to make. Sad.

For the refreshing company they offered me, the endless chats we shared, for the visits they accompanied me on, for all their time and patience with me, I thank Saroja and Karthi. I learnt more about art from them than I could ever hope to teach them.

For those sweaty mornings we spent working together on cataloging, her sweet way of humming while we were at it, I shall remember Then. I hope the kids still adore her like they did when I was there, and I hope they don't test her patience as much!

For all those fresh conversations laced with a rustic wit, for all the profound knowledge about various fields that he imparted to me, I shall remember Ponnudurai Sir. I hope his daughter, Ahalya, is doing fine and that his wife's scanning has shown good results...For all those evenings that I spent running behind her, I shall remember my first ever cycle student... I hope Mallika is doing well. Tell her I want my ride with her, as a pillion, on her cycle the next time I visit!

For those evenings that we spent scraping the violin, the guffaws we shared about extinct species, the little nothings in our evenings, the delicious parting lunch that she and her mum prepared for us, the pleasant and patient, the haunting trademark smile of hers, I shall remember Mythili. I hope this multi-faceted lady has been practicing sketching. Have you, Mythili?

To all those refreshing coffees that she took special efforts to brew just for me, to all those mouthwatering dishes she indulged me with, to all the motherly love and affection that she gave me... I shall forever remain indebted to Jayamma. I hope she has learnt to sign her name right now. Somebody please tell her I miss the coffees' she used to brew me in the kitchen, after freshly cleaning the place with cow-dung-mixed-water!

To those endless engaging conversations that captured my days effortlessly, to all those narration filled evenings that seemed ever too short for me to let go, to all the borrowed eccentricities that I can add to my own character henceforth, to all those enthusiastic pursuits that he set me unto, to all the glorious moments that he managed to spare for me despite his time being too expensive to be spent on trifles like me, to have taught me just about every lesson that I have learnt during my stay there and for opening my vision to capture new perspectives of life that I had never seen existing before... to all of these and much more, I can barely thank Senthil enough. He is 'THE' magic charm behind Payir... the wonderful man who can ceaselessly manage to keep you in awe of him!

Besides, I hope SKG (NOT the founder!) Sir's daughter is doing well. Manohar Sir, I hope he is not as busy as Senthil usually keeps him! Gajendran Sir, I hope he has been hunting as much as he likes. I hope Soubhagyam Ma'am and Selvaraj Sirare keeping well... And, how are the folks in the Chutti school and the BPO?

I can only wish they're all keeping well... and that I shall!

My Spiritual Companion
Finally, without realizing the plans of the Divine Nature...I fell in love with Preeti who supported in various projects. My marriage was made in heaven as

I had no intentions of getting married at any point of my career, happening at the same place that brought Preeti and me together as also many of us. Who knows what the Divine plans are for each of us. I tied the knot of oat into a Divine relationship. Where the man has pronounced a woman as his wife...to support her and praise her for what she his..as an embodiment of the Divine Nature

As my wedding invitation read in the facebook....

'Payir farm is also an ideal getaway for you during this holiday. That is only a cue as you always know me...Yuppies. We need help with the marriage preparation!!!..so,...just drop a word and we will make arrangements for your stay and plan your volunteer time'

Directions to the venue:

Buses from Trichy Chattiram to Thenur village (via T.Kalathur bound Thuraiyur):

04:20 am Sumathi Bus Service 08:40 am G. Vijay.
06:30 am Saraswathi 09:40 am Sumathi Bus Service.
07:20 am DCTC (Govt. Bus) 11:40 am Saraswathi.

Buses from Thuraiyur to Thenur village (via T.Kalathur) runs every hour.

I met Aparna who was selected as part of an NGO. iVolunteer IFY Programme in 2010, an information science and engineering student from Bangalore, as one of the candidates who got through the initial scanning process. After many weeks of eager waiting, I finally found myself aboard the train to Trichy - all set to spend a month volunteering with Payir Trust. A beautiful young woman from Bangalore who had visited us in the year 2010

J: 'Aparna, How do you find this place. You do not have an AC? And a nice car that you drive back in Bangalore'

"Oh no..I am enjoying my time out here with the morning birds and the alliance with Nature working in the field gives me some exercise; perhaps, this is what I have been looking for long...Payir has made an impact in my life as it did with several thousands of families around as I see during the Aid season in 2010

about my first day gave me sufficient hints about how the rest of my stay there would be like. To the unmatched, unsurpassed hospitality that I was smothered with, the selfless ability of the folks there to adapt to anybody and make people feel like they have always belonged there, to all those wonderful people who have touched my life in ways that I cannot forget, to all the memories that I have managed to capture from these few days and to everything that has changed about me since my visit here, I shall forever remain indebted to Payir!

*

The Friends of Payir (FoP) have extended the wings to Bangalore, the IT corridor of India, which has exemplified its presence by leveraging the social media with a few volunteers those who plans ahead to keep it moving across metropolis, especially I would like to thank my frriends of Payir chapter for taking tasks to completion..It was a project and yet another milestone in taking Payir in a methodological way of approaching the corporates with the key anchors listed below supporting varying topics:

Key Anchors:
1. Ram along with Ravi and Thirunavukkarasu for Donation drive.
2. Kanchana for Volunteer Program.
3. Sathish for Task List.
4. T Kuppuswamy for Translation.
5. Payir website : Vidhya

SBCF Awareness Program
SKG is a man who has connected technology to the villages, riding a bicycle carrying a laptop wired to the rest of the world, who has put the village of

Thenur to the rest of the world. I hear that every time 'Technology is a means to help you all'

Is it so.as the multimillion dollar projects have not succeeded to the extent of food for all? The caveat is that only a limited few have managed to find projects and it continue with the link of upper middle classes, probably to some extent middle classes have prospered by the technology, however the plight of the villages remain the same.

SKG demonstrated that 'leadership' – Leading by example from the front with the technology power points, engineering in wireless technology and civil engineering by constructing low cost houses for the villagers…and contemporary farming techniques. And many more as the projects list almost extend every year as the projects started with education to the computer technology for the poor with more than ten desktops installed in the lab.

It is not just feeding the poor. Indeed it is a broader vision of empowering each one of them…in to leaders of tomorrow with the cancer awareness programs…welfare of the women program etc. and the list is extending beyond

Education, Health care and computers!!!! With the skill development program to help youth from addictions to the skillful resources. And the women to just the household stuff to the technology and communication

A local villager could speak little bit of English

A local village kid asked

"How are you sir?"

I am fine thank you as I replied

'Pleasure is mine…as it came crisp with the tender hands offering me a tender coconut with love'

Whats your name girl? Sir, my name is Veena…Veena is an intelligent girl with her father was affected with HIV, who was admitted at the hospital. When the entire community did not support Veena, and her mom…SKG did support wholeheartedly to save the child from the mental torture. She is just fine, above all she is our child my friends as he spoke aloud to the meeting, reminding me of the freedom fighter V.O.Chidambaram Pillai of pre-Independence days

She is our child pa….let's take care as he walked adding another one to the Payir community.

Chapter 5 MY VISION PAYIR 2020

I was constantly reminded by the ideals of Swami Vivekanda, Mahatma Gandhi and Buddha. The ideals of truth, and compassion, have helped me in forging the ideals of Payir.

While Vivekananda was driven by the ideology of changes inner, the conducive environment is required with the basic needs to be fulfilled, hence, I decided to start at the grass roots of humanity to empower communities as my observation is that basic needs to be fulfilled as a priority

I would like to remind you of the Mahakavi Bharti, a great Tamil poet who has opined:

Let us destroy the World

If there is no food for even an individual

From time immemorial, India has produced the greatest thinkers of times such as Buddha, Mahatma Gandhi and poets such as Tagore, Bharti those who contributed to the spiritual growth as well as the freedom movement during the pre-Independence country

Perhaps a similar revolution is required, and this time it is not against anyone, it is to join hands with each of you to form the one-hand Governance to support each other in the journey of consciousness

As a primary factor, our wealth is not distributed. In the 18th century, Karl Marx was instrumental in forming the principles of socialism, where in a real democracy each of your basic needs taken care in a democratic Nation. I have witnessed it in the United States, which has every reason to be the best country in the world with robust Governance. The Eastern countries such as India has intelligence, however the democracy seem to have taken a back seat with a few corrupt politicians and lack of Governance to be able to implement measures to support individuals, resulting in funds not reaching the individuals for the welfare of humanity

I feel in a similar context, most part of Africa despite Natural resources, seems to have gone below the level of poverty with malnutrition children dying out of hunger every year. One of my visions is to extend the model of micro-economy to every village in the world to support these communities in their growth and self-reliance.

It is your birth right to claim fulfillment of basic needs, if a Government is unable to provide it. It is a definite failure of democracy. Payir envisages the transformation of Indian villages into a socially stimulating, self-reliant, growth oriented community rooted in the principles of Truth - a society where people practice and interact with the highest moral values.

The belief that every human-being deserves a good quality of life is the driving force of the Payir Ashram - a rural empowerment facilitation center, henceforth termed as Payir.

We will work in rural villages of India to create an atmosphere where people have the space to practice truth. We will lead, create opportunities, facilitate and mentor. We will take a holistic development approach touching all aspects of the society - be it local economy and revenue, social needs like health; education; sanitation; infrastructure, civic and panchayat systems and also spiritual needs.

We will not only understand and facilitate work for the identified needs of the current society but more importantly lead with a foresight into the future growth of the society. Through the entire process, we will partner with the local populace and nurture leaders among them for eventual take over. We believe in the realization of the fundamentals of Panchayat Raj as envisaged by Gandhi.

Any community should be able to own the ideas that are needed for their continuous development — be it their physical, civic or spiritual. Owning of the ideas means collectively create new thoughts and create/manage resources to implement and execute it. At the individual level, each individual should be able to self-realize his/her own potentials, without any distinction based upon caste or creed. This would in essence mean to build an environment where even the most ordinary person lives with self-respect

When I enquired about the plans for the future, it was even more astounding…as S.K.G's contemporary plans for the future taking the world beyond:

"I am intending to providing a conducive environment for children, women and adults. A robust governance of Panchayat to implement with transparency in spending in every phase of the project implementation. The micro economy is concerned with how supply and demand interact in individual markets for goods and services. Did you ever think about the unfair, uneven economics? And the inequality in someone in the cities making money vs. relatively a poor farmer who works harder through the day;

I did not want to interrupt as the theories of Karl Marx was imminent from the modest person of

Thenur in a dhoti, portraying the principles of Gandhism.

Jay: Well S.K.G. 'What is the pragmatic approach?'

S.K.G: The pragmatic approach is to analyze the current economic reforms and by empowering village panchayats and enabling more transparency can elevate the communities in villages. Next most important point is to provide enough funding's to help them self-sustain without too much of dependencies.

The basics of good education, schools and infrastructure and inter-connectivity to the villages are a must like in the United States. This would create more jobs and rapid migration of students to other cities and deploy contemporary farming techniques to boost productivity

There is a lot more …

Ok. As I interrupted S.K.G for a while for a short break to complete the hot servings of cookies with a nice cup of brewed coffee reminding our stay in the United States.

As S.K.G continued non-stop with the future plans with a plan chalked out in the board. And the finances was a concern as the organization is primarily funded by friends and some well-wishers which is not going to sustain the growth of the community with the ever increasing needs of projects and funding needs by the way of corporate funding or the Government project funding. Either way we are ready to partner with the major corporates in adopting villages as we have 700,000 thousand villages it will need stupendous efforts in next few decades to transform

Finally, if you ever need India to be a great Nation in the world arena, villages have to be empowered and self-reliant. The vision of Payir for 2020 is to cover villages in south and north-east with the recent disaster of Uttarkhand is inflicting pain in my heart for the welfare of people in the North eastern part of India. Beyond 2020 if Divine Nature wants us beyond the shores, I am prepared and I will be able to take Payir to several million households in the African continent

Swami Vivekananda was trying to change the fate of poverty in India by educating the masses through the spiritual empowerment

Give me hundred men; I will change the World

As I thought; It is deeply saddening to see the psychological maturity of a few who intervene and interrogate the motto of organizations which are contemporary with small Panchayat's challenging the vision of Payir

But S.K.G was relentless in his goals, despite the discouraging words of some of the localities to the Government officials, he continued with available funds and the overseas connections through friends and families extending his Bangalore chapter of Payir rolled out in the year 2010. All good things will expand; no matter how much opposition exist, as Nature will continue to exercise her will

It was a perfect cast of the Mother Nature in her gracious eyes opened towards ignorant villagers. Though, if you do not support; perhaps you should refrain from hurting the vision, and goals.

In spite of all these challenges, S.K.G is working toward the common goal of empowering villages and the rest all is secondary

From the circle of social community expanding through the media such as Facebook, across the shores of India and overseas in connections with Asha foundation of the United States.

Each village should be made self-reliant with less or no dependencies, let the cities ride on the villages and not the other way. The native swadeshi products should compete in global standards with required subsidies and every MNC organization must be resorting to adapting a village for a certain tax-rebate, which would be entitled

If someone is working abroad, the following family should pay FT. Foreign Trade tax or Foreign work tax which would go to the village budget for the development of required infrastructure in the villages. Thus, it can be balanced and further by the way of sharing work with the software organizations extending its secondary arms in the towns, funded and supported by the governmental organization is a must to-do activity to sustain the rural empowerment policies. Let these good rules be established as amendments to the constitution and every citizen of this country should be eligible for the social security fund to sustain mounting economic issues and reforms

The roots of wisdom is expanding, thus driving all ignorance in the mankind to strive for joining hands for creating a community where women, and children are safe with the basic needs fulfilled in every villages; above all a tribute to Mahatma Gandhi
For this gentle man in his ardent style of body, mind and spirit dedicated to the welfare of people and a great community which was in the brink of absolute destruction

The classical Shivaji the warrior has arrived in the village of Thenur, a Chola kingdom once is now the onus of draught weather conditions. I hope the Chola warrior can take the village of Thenur with the emerging Doctors, Scientists and Engineers.

A silent revolution has just begun!!!!
A silent revolution has just begun!!!!

Oh my dear brothers, and sisters, open your eyes and ears of wisdom with heart filled in love to support humanity to strive in success in empowering villages.

Let's join hands to support this great organization and the vision of Payir is every Indian's dream.

Often times it reminded me of Mr.Thomson and his rules and messages to carry forward, which later changed my life forever. These incidences were fresh in my memory, as though it happened a few minutes ago;

'I was determined to campaign for the Panchayat elections to support over a thousand families to expand the mode to all neighboring villages…' Anna..Neenga election la nikkanoom to help more number of people as I registered my name for the Panchayat elections

It was early in the morning…as I usually wake up at four in the morning for my prayers and planning the work for the day. There were three men with masks who lit fire in the Organic farm..and they sent an intimidating courier with a message to stop contesting as my interest grew larger to contest…After intense campaign, the results were not in my favor. I was rather thinking more about people's expectations as you cannot assume anything.

However, Thuraisammy and his friends of my school indicated something went on at the electorate which they cited few lakhs spent by the opposition party. I related this to the former incidence to find there could be something fishy…I didn't want any unpleasant issues amidst good things and progress with PAYIR as I continued with my reforms with my own sources.

But the above incidents have kept me vibrating in my mind..why would someone disrupt in humanity services and the answer was the animal instincts in humans have not been resolved yet which is a constant conflict in most of them, resorting to measures of crime; with a vow of not to identify these young men whom I have identified

As I opened the scribbling in the package in Tamil. It was written with some grammatical errors which gave me a clue of who had done this…I want to teach you a lesson for your election campaign was written in the local language…

Vungalluku oru pahdam katho tharuveyan…instead it was written as 'padam' which is a frequent error as I traced back in all seven schools to find a similar age group of students who are making these mistakes

Ayah. Can you identify who has similar mistakes' as the teachers had convened to confess on how many of these students are making such mistakes. SKG narrowed down a few, and finally a group of three men from the same school 'PENNADAM HSC' ok. He called these men…he knew them by eyes as they were struggling to stand in front of his piercing eyes.

Like a lion he stood in front of them…Pasangala, what did you do.

Saar, naanga yedhuvum seyala…what? (we did not do anything)

Is it so..where is your sister in the hospital for treatment. Just think what has helped her my son... Saar. My sister's operation is fine because of your hospital and my mom is happy as my sis has regained her vision...

Durai "You don't know how much we funded for the operation" it came from all the hard work of one week efforts which yielded only ten thousand which I kept to pay the salary for all our employees. Now, that I paid for your sis' operation. With no money in hand...what am I do

Saar 'yenna manichidonga saar' (I am so sorry) with rolling tears in his cheeks..

Yampa...Yampa why are you doing this?

Saar. Pannayar yennaku ayiram roobai kodutharoo. The rich man in town bribed me Rs.1000 one thousand rupees to destroy the farm! And others joined him and fell under my feet., as a token of reverence and sorry state

What am I do? Why world is against me

At first I lost the elections, and second I could not save a yearlong efforts going waste in the farm overnight...and the cattle are all infected by virus. As I stood up to let me emotions go...with the open skies and dry farm land and failed agriculture with my dhoti finding its solace on the ground feeling its warmth.

Just let it go. Today was not yours but tomorrow will be yours. Just get up and do your deed!!!!

The resounding truths with a copy of Bhagwat Geetha talking to me which I have not read through for months as I bought it from the book store in Trichy…

'Do your duty

I will yield as results"

The above statement as uttered by Krishna…to Arjun ahead of the deadly war of Gurushethra..

Kannan ' I find my nephews, my cousins and brothers in front of me…how can I find courage to find against them as my heart is melting away in love'

Arjun 'It is not you who ride' as I do and it is all my manifestations. Each of them is part of me including you and there is no one who is away from me'

'Just do your duty, as I'd yield as results'

I have read through the duty consciousness and Swami Vivekananda's speech in Chicago was significant addressing the entire group of professionals as 'Brothers and Sisters' the entire group listened to the next one hour where he walked them through the core principles of Vedanta. And the part is God's manifestations in the universal brotherhood as he concluded the speech with a foray of love and affection from the fellow beings in the United States, the land of opportunities.

As I just reflected on these statements. My failures were too little and too insignificant as I decided to plan for seeking more sponsorship...On that day, I wrote a memorandum:

'My dear friends and families. I strive hard for success to help every villager success. As Mahatma said every village should be empowered, and every child should deserve the best of the education. Payir has foundation pillars of education, jobs for adults, women empowerment and spiritual growth as a holistic plan for each individual across the Globe. I am not going to ask for sponsors. If you do will for something to support for a cause. Of course you can. Contact me SKG...as I signed the letter and send it to many people whom I know'

The first response was from a foundation called 'Asha' which his predominantly started by the elite group of men and women from India, those who have settled in the United States.

The response was overwhelming with over a hundred response with intense care and love from overseas through the job connections, and my school connection which had fetched some money to survive and repair the damage caused in the Organic farm and treat the cattle

The mother as I call her…cattle was just lying down with high fever and in India; It is a sign of ominous and a bad omen to let the cow die. As I called off for a vet. He injected and gave some medications

'Lakshmi ma. As I called her 'Lakshmi ma…open your eyes as she was suffering from high temperature and I called the vet once again.

The vet hospital finally sent a young nurse to administer some injections to the cow and take care..

Nila her name in twenties working as a nurse in the vet clinic. She was passionate and beautiful with brown eyes for her age of impeccable rigor!!!

"Sar. What is the problem for her? As she passionately touched the Lakshmi ma"

She is sick and has very high temperature

No problem saar. I have treated many Lakshmi's in her smile. As she smiles at me. Ok. Then treat her now and take care of her for next couple of days. Where do I stay…

Here In the cow dung as Lakshmi ma will need you anytime. Just keep an eye on her.

Saar ..there is a lot of mosquitos.

Ok ok. Don't cry. Rest there in my room. I will wake up if Lakshmi ma needs you. Ok

The next morning. Nila, Nila, the sun is up for a long time. Why are you Nila (moon) resting as you promised to save Lakshmi ma (cow)...sorry sar. I was a little tired last night due to travel in last couple of days. Ok ok

Get up and have your breakfast.

Cheeee. Just a porridge. Come on girl, this is kambu koozh good for health a nutritious drink. Have it and get back to job.

she was ready in about half an hour and then took charge in her regular attire of a nurse with stethoscope to check the heartbeat of Lakshmi ma...

Nila, how is she doing? A lot better after the first set of medications. Well . sorry

What? I forgot to inject her last night some chloroform to alleviate from pain? I did that...

What saar ? yes. I have spent few weeks in the cattle farm and I know how to inject and administer medicines. She was touched by his gentleness and not wanting to escalate the matter to the hospital

Lakshmi ma was perfectly fine after a couple of days ..

I was reading through the verses of Kamba about Hindu epic Ramayana where he says

'She looked down from the balcony

Where eyes meet of that of Rama

For a split second of aligned consciousness'

It was a love at the first sight of my consciousness

Like a rising sun as I felt current wave in myself;

As I concluded this chapter, I found her ….perhaps the destiny was calling me to find her as I loved her wittiness and etiquette of serving the poor. She was on a college vacation, as a project to support the education of poor children ..she taught

Akka 'puriyala' cannot understand

She was patient enough to repeat complex math problems and science as she became a full time teacher. She forget her semester project, apparently as her project became integral part of her life. And my life as well

She is like the women of Bharti ..as he claimed

"Born are the women to win

Defy the wisdom of shyness and be bold

To win hearts of wisdom"

She is a good Carnatic singer, where my heart finds its solace. Perhaps an angel as I'd recall sent by God to support me in renovating villages with an image of

Global picture not by just feeding them, perhaps by bringing out leaders of future generations. I would like to strive for globalizing food, and water as the common and basic needs of humans are same anywhere in the world. Indeed it is the greed that makes it difficult. Nature is by itself democratic as the needs are same, only it varies in quanta based on your relentless desires without boundaries.

As I refer to my archives of my plans…of course most of it has materialized with the interim hard ships:

The Road map found in my archives during the yester years of 2005-2008….when PAYIR was on paper.

Project Payir – Road Map

I had developed the Project Payir road map almost a decade ago when I was studying and my thoughts were forged based on sequence of events that had influenced on my way. Project Payir's goal is to facilitate people to create a society that thrives on Truth. Truth is an all embodiment word for satisfaction of all senses, pure actions, knowledge, peace and happiness. Truth is the attainment of moral, spiritual, social and intellectual goal of each and every person in this society, by his or her own actions.

Payir is to provide that opportunity to this people. This is surely not the first project to have been implemented in this world with the same goals. This has been the goals of many a virtuous human being, even before Gita was told. My goal is to take one more such journey to achieve this society of Truth. I have dedicated my life to the success of this project.

The aim of this document is to describe my road map, concentrating on a major detail towards my commitment to this project.

Road Map I will be returning to India by October 2004. I intend to start a hospital and renovate the primary school at my village, Sathanoor. Sathanoor is a small village 40 kms south east of Trichy. Sathanoor has about 200 families (~1000 people) and has about 5-6 neighboring villages with about the same population. The hospital will be a 10-bed hospital, with 3 one-bed rooms a nd 2 three-bed rooms, each with an attached bath and toilet. (Single beds are provided on medical needs basis and not based on any other criteria). The hospital will have an Operation Theatre/Emergency Care Unit and a consultation room. The hospital will also house a laboratory and a pharmacy. The Operation Theatre /ER will service critical illness and non-specialty surgery. All specialty surgery and treatment will be transferred to a hospital in Trichy, when the patient is transportable.

The hospital will have 2 resident doctors, a general physician and a pediatrician; one male and one female nurse; a lab cum pharmacy technician. There would at least be 2 consulting doctors, a gynecologist and a surgeon, with visitation on a weekly or as needed basis. Later on, medical camps will be conducted at the hospital.

An ambulance, equipped with first aid care, will be available for service, 24 x 7, at the hospital. A driver, who will work part-time at the farm, will be assigned for the ambulance. I will initially conduct the overall administration of the hospital. This would include hospital building; financial and human resource mobilization; and up-keep. Sathanoor already has a primary school with classes' up to 5thgrade. Currently, the school is not functioning at the standards it should. It is just a noon meal center to describe at the best. The class rooms are either dysfunctional or operating at very low student capacity. This is the case with at least two other neighboring villages and rest of the villages does not have a primary education center.

To address this, the school's existing building will be renovated to create a better educational environment. A library will be added to the school. Initially, the library will have books, educational material that will be required for the students/kids. Later on, this will be augmented with books for adult education. 3 good teachers will be recruited to teach the Native language, Tamil; English and Science.

I will be teaching Mathematics. A school bus or a transportation vehicle will be owned by the school to commute the school students between the different villages. Also, the project team will address with the local government about free educational material to individual students and proper and well maintained noon-meal scheme. It will also work to augment the school till Grade 8 within 1 year into this project. This would be the initial setup with which I will start my project. I plan to stabilize these tasks by December 2006. During 2007 and 2008, I will concentrate on addressing the agricultural practices in the village and facilitating village development works as identified by government and non-profit non-governmental programs to be actually carried out by the local people – a program of "beneficiaries reap based on self-participation.

From this point onwards, I have two paths planned, one of which will be decided by December

2007. During this journey, I would form a team of dedicated people who share the same ideology. The two paths can be broadly classified as spiritual or political . Spiritual would be to extend the above structure and system to multiple villages, initially in Tamil Nadu and later throughout India. The political path would be to involve in local government making at the initial stages and later move on as necessitated for and by the project. Based on my initial discussions with well-wishers to the project, who include experienced doctors, socialists, elders who attained success in their own way in life and some of you, here is my financial estimate and an achievement plan.

Hospital
- Land and Building: Rs. 6 Lakhs
- Equipment's (as far as possible, good used ones): Rs.8 Lakhs
- Ambulance (Second Hand): Rs.5 Lakhs
- Resource Mobilization: Rs.1 Lakh
- First 6 month running cost: Rs.1.5 Lakhs

School
- School Renovation: Rs. 1.5 Lakh
- Library: Rs. 0.5 Lakh
- School Bus: 3 Lakh (used Mini-van)
- First 6 month running cost: Rs.0.5 Lakhs
- I would have a saving of US$ 50,000 by Oc
- tober 2004, which converts to about 25 Lakh rupees. I will need 1 Lakh for setting up
- my agricultural farm. I am working on to address the short fall of about 3 lakhs between the project cost and my savings.
- Challenges- Here I have addressed (in rather lengthy manner) some of the challenges in achieving this goal. Many of these have been brought by you, during my discussions.

*

Decisive Politics

I have ventured in to politics ever since I was thinking about welfare of the villages. I did not want to shy away from the governance or Panchayat responsibilities. I would like to contest in elections to help the people of my country to bring the change in every villages, unless I have the consistent inflow in the way of charity through the government funds. It will be difficult. I would like to change North Eastern villages of India and beyond the shores of India in every villages in Africa where Gandhiji had his foot print. I would ensure each village would prosper in finally forming one Global Village with seamless integration with cities and towns. Let us share the prosperity as Karl Marx highlighted. It will not be an imposed communism. First time in the history a paradigm shift in socialism blossoming in every part of the world with the common land for all to share. As we have Nature providing us the same resources to utilize, and why do we create boundaries.

Globalizing Food, Water & work hours (rest)

I believe every human is very unique and endowed with the eternal consciousness; this would help us understand the basic needs of food, water, which are common needs of every individual. Hence, I would call God is the super Democrat who has planned everyone to share the resources that he has bestowed

My goal is to discuss with the UNESCO and the Belinda GATES foundation who take care of many projects in the Africa continent to demonstrate the

challenges that we have in every country and formalize the resolution plan in the summit. Often times I have observed people do not know what they want, hence it is imperative for the World government organizations such as UNESCO to implement steps to share the Natural resources such as free food, water and work hours with free education for all. These are all natural utilities, then why should anyone pay for it and to whom should we pay? If at all, we should pay to the super GOD the creator who is showering as rain, and light in sun shine and breeze. What can you pay the eternal?

Magudam-2011 Event in Payir School
The events conducted in the Payir schools are always colorful with the Dream India Org. conducted events in 2011 with competition and prizes to children, celebrating Gandhi Jayanthi. The Magudam-2011 was a big success with every child demonstrating her skill in dancing, art and science competition

There were 12 schools participated with over 1100 children. Our Payir team started the preparations at least one month before the event by conducting prelims for all the events at various schools. Habib, Mythili and others from Payir team did a wonderful job by conducting all these

We had the Finals on this day. Payir team had completed the prelims and we had 5 teams participate. Children answered very well. Special mention should be made of children who recognized Mr.Obama's & Mr.Sachin's voice in the Audio round.

This again showed that rural kids can actually compete very well with urban kids. The audience too had their chances and did well.

Our Prize distribution was followed by couple of cultural show by children. A small kid who danced to tune of hip hop stole the thunder. She was absolutely amazing that whole audience including the collector started clapping all through the song. Another kid delivered a wonderful speech on "Confidence".

The collector asked the children to make use of such opportunities and promised provide all support required from his side. Various other government officials too spoke on this occasion with a few encouraging children to dream about "Dream India" inspired by Dr.APJ.

Dream India would like to convey special thanks to the entire Payir team
>> for the wonderful work. Special thanks to Ms.Mythili, Mr.Habib and Mr.Pachamuthu for their wonderful work. execution of the whole event was fantastic. Dream India is proud and happy to be associated with Payir team lead by Mr.Senthil and conduct this event every year.

As I recollect my special thanks to Action2020 group that brought us all together. It was a dream comes true. Most importantly these children were feeling connected and motivated to do more. This is one way of connecting to the communities, especially children.

Action 2020 meeting with the former Indian President, APJ

The energy was exuberant and the wisdom of the former Mr.President in his ardent style, encouraging our plans by reviewing it to the details.

"Life if a challenge...let you live through it and help others" nalla vishayam thambi let me know if you need help anywhere. Keep it going from the world renowned scientist from the lands of Rameshwaram.

On the 7th October 2009, former Indian President Dr A P J Abdul Kalam met 70 representatives from 30 constituent organisations of Action 2020 Team or online India Vision Group at Chennai. Dr Kalam spent nearly two hours with the members sharing his views. At the end of his 30 minute speech, all the members were highly motivated with positive energy. Thereafter he spent his time taking questions from the members and guiding them for Nation building.

EPILOGUE

My journey had started from the time I read Swami
Vivekanada, Paramahamsa and Mahatma Gandhi.
And my dreams forged with my spiritual encounters
with Mr. Thompson and the sequence of events that
followed after that is just the conscious trip to serve
the humanity. Whatever is possible? To alleviate the
sufferings of humanity in education a child as I had
started with brought in tremendous joy and helped
me in expanding further. Eventually it ended in the
foundation called 'PAYIR' with a motto of
illuminating children, and empowers rural areas
which have had tremendous success, despite Indian
map in the Global scenario as an IT hub.

Each of you have the ability to identify the sufferings
around you. There is a lot more that you can do
through your relentless work by sharing the
knowledge, educating poor children to the possible
extent, as monetary benefits alone is not a service.
Perhaps you should start from your nearest
surroundings in alleviating the sufferings

This is an invitation of realizing the values of
humanity. After all the ordeal, Buddha had returned
back to the community to help the poorest of the poor,
despite born as an Emperor of a large Kingdom. You
might have heard about Emperor Ashoka who had
embraced Buddhism after the deadly war of Kalinga,
and the history will continue of Martyrs wisdom….

In Mahatma Gandhi who had transformed the entire society in the movement of '**Ahimsa**', the non-violence moment in a silent rebellion.

The post-Independent era of over fifty years have industrialized our country with the permanent space in the Global economy, however the backbone of India, Our Villages still remains the same. The villages and the panchayat system are not empowered enough to help the livelihood of poor villagers, resulting in malnourished children, jobless adults, and careless youth who turn criminals without proper health care centers

The future of India resides in the hands of younger generation. If they are not empowered through the way of proper education, the country will not succeed in its dreams

The tele medicine, micro economy is a model practiced by Payir with the combination of technology and Governance with transparency. These are value based systems for the future Governance which can be practices anywhere in the world

I believe Payir is not to be concluded as another community service NGO within the boundaries of the country. It is a beginning of a **Silent Revolution** of human consciousness looking forward to prosperity of fulfilling its basic needs as the birth right, and helps the communities transform spiritual in the yearning consciousness to reach itself to the fullest. After all in the journey of consciousness is to help each other, transcend mundane plane of life in reaching the Divine Nature.

The ancient revolutions have been in terms of evolving of human culture, society in socialism, communism and religionism. It is a beginning of a Silent Revolution in transforming communities to self-reliant society with conducive environment for children by providing best healthcare services,

When the dreams grow larger. The consciousness evolves as the human minds are unleashed to reach to the mars. And it should not be an endeavor to just fulfilling its needs. The Payir trust is an organization to fulfilling the basic needs of human consciousness and beyond to reach the Divine Nature in every village, country and the World

My dream of the World is one Global Village as the needs are common, and Nature is a democrat. There is no need to prove through stronger borders or the army to promote peace. If the individuals transform, the societies will transform, and eventually countries will transform. It will need tremendous courage, and transformation and each of you are the crop the 'PAYIR' in exact terms to grow consciously supporting alleviating pains of fellow human beings anywhere in the World. Whether it is in Africa or India or anywhere in the World, Payir is determined to look beyond the shores to reaching out to the common Man.

In my observation each human being is born with unique talent, perhaps he or she may not have had the right opportunity to excel due to lack of opportunity provided. Most of these children in villages are intelligent enough as they grasp things quickly like a soft mold, that can perhaps be molded for a better humanity. The country's well-being depends in its youth, and the generations look up to the willingness of younger generations to contribute towards the welfare of the society

If you have all basic needs fulfilled, work toward helping the poor. If you are poor, work toward reaching a minimal state of self-reliance, without depending in the Government, as you will need to build your skill development at an early age without wasting your youth. The power of youth is like unleashing a atomic energy; If harnessed properly, a Nation can transform, perhaps the world can look forward to a better and universal culture with oneness and the universal brotherhood

It is possible through your ability to interlink rivers across the boundaries; it is possible if you strive a little harder to build one Global culture in the vanishing boundaries of one-Governance. It is possible if you just sow the seed now in your thinking, no need to do anything. Just think and bless the world towards Universal brotherhood. The Divine Nature will cast her show with the right people arriving on time as the 'Incredible Messiah' of the world.

Today Thenur has a messiah, a Shivaji the warrior of contemporary world who rides a bicycle carrying a laptop, thus connecting his Organization to the world. In a simple attire, with profound responsibilities that the world largest democracy has failed to provide.

It is an invitation to the bold youth as Vivekananda said. Not just the hundred. We need thousands of them to form communities to support rural empowerment, through the urban realization of our backbone. None should be left out without food or basic needs fulfilled with the principles of helping others in eliminating pains, as the need of the hour of humanitarian services.

I am sure each of you have read through my journey, every expansion of mind is an expansion of your vision and my story is your story too. Just you have to observe sequence of events a little closely to find the ultimate journey. You are not born to be alone, in a social setup and humanity and consciousness is all interlinked.

You were endowed with consciousness and more service that you do would help you in spiritual journey. You will need to transform from the ordinary circumstances to the extraordinary events of success and goodness as you ponder in each of your life's incidents.

Above all, I reckon in this journey of our short life-span is to reflect deeply in to ourselves. With a plan to support each other consciously in the evolution of human consciousness. I am sure each of you would transform your life by helping each other. Let us not wait for any disaster to help you tie up humanity. It is your inherent Nature, just nurture it and the messages of Mr. Thompson have been delivered to you. I wish you would take it forward with you and multiply happiness, peace and prosperity

If you too goal oriented, the inner consciousness becomes a vacuum and you would feel something is missing through the life-time endeavor. Your life is not something to be wasted in just few mundane tasks; it has to expand as it is intended for expanding yourself to the consciousness, and supporting each other.

The moment you think about helping others, Nature will help you with seven steps to reach up there. The Divine doors would open up for you when your heart is filled with love, and devotion.

Let the revolution of **Payir** begin as your inner revolution, in transforming and empowering the communities in each of these countries not bound by the barricades of man-made boundaries. For you and me we are just one and the same; in transforming political situations to the polite situations by the way of educating the youth to transform the mundane plane of earth to the eternal life with peace and prosperity with over a billion smiles in each of you. Before I conclude, I just reminded by the words of the Divine Mr. Thompson who said:

"'Do not stop. Until I hear the last child on earth stops crying" and let Vijay ma's story be the past..and my meetings with Mr.Thomas striking my inner chords of wisdom"

It was a paradox, a parable as he did not want me to stop. From the time I started listening to the facts of Payir, researching each of its success and need of the humanity was just flashing as visions in my mind with open hearts. Often times you enclose your minds into the corridors of projects boundaries and you do not seem to be expanding beyond it within the walls of the IT infrastructure. As Buddha asked for alms 'Bodhi Bikshanthi' every day, every morning asking for alms for reminding you of the birth-right of enlightenment, every one. Each of you rest of his life. The peak of consciousness in saints, and seers have finally ended up in the humanity in treating each of you as Divine to support in basic needs from Saint Vallalar to Valluvar.

I would like to thank each of you reading my journey, and I am going to ask for supporting the good cause of elevating poorest of the poor children of the world to be educated from the illness of conditioned minds to the expanded state of consciousness, with the basic needs of humans fulfilled. It is everyone's birth right to fulfill needs which is spiritual and a social responsibility, as God didn't intend to keep you poor, only the greedy politicians. Let the PAYIR's vision beyond to support the empowerment of your children for a bright future in every village, country in the world as one Global Village.

Acknowledgements

I'd like to thank Mr. S.K.G (Senthil Kumar Gopalan) for his time in narrating events of significance and time taken to proof-read the manuscript to entirety.

I salute his responsibility and my earnest hope to S.K.G to win the upcoming Panchayat elections to implement the policies and his life time ordinance to support rural empowerment as an integral part of Panchayat tasks. Payir is one of the few Organizations in the world with a vision of rural empowerment; it has plans to educate children in rural areas in Trichy. But not limited to Trichy, it is extending its wings of wisdom with Bangalore chapters

There are plans such as tele-mobile, healthcare program for all and jobs for adults are part of the responsibilities of the Panchayat in villages. I am astounded with Individuals accomplishments in Payir which is empowering an entire community in the village of Thenur, Trichy

I thank for his time and efforts and I salute for all his sacrifices and I pray to the Divine Nature who is casting his play. Indeed a step well taken will progress in a country where the democracy is failing. Mr. S.K.G is an entrepreneur, social activist and an astute business man with his plans to empower the community, village and the Nation.
I pray to the Divine Nature for the great souls such as S.K.G to ride the wave to succeed.

Award "Highest Rotary Award"
At the award ceremony at the Taj Connemara, Tamil
Nadu Tourism Secretary V. Irai Anbu applauded the
Gandhian nature of Senthil Kumar's vision of making
India better by improving her villages, and called for
more public support of projects like Payir.

The Madras Esplanade Rotary Club's president, K.
Govindarajan, chanced upon a magazine article about
Payir's activities, and was moved to visit Thenur
along with his Rotary associates, he said. "Most of us
have no idea about conditions in villages," he said.
Figuring that since they couldn't contribute their
personal efforts, the least they could do was to help
someone who could, club members have thrown their
support behind Payir.

The club will sponsor several requirements for the
school set up by Payir, including a roofing sheet and
clothes for children. Besides, it will also collect and
donate clothes for women and organize and support
medical camps in the village. Inspired by Senthil
Kumar's work, the club has adopted the
Kuthambakkam
village near Chennai, and has earmarked Rs. 10 lakh
for rural development. Senthil Kumar praised the
Rotary's Club diligence in "finding" him and
approaching him to offer their support. He used the
platform to highlight the perpetual paucity of funds
in organizations such as his, and urged the audience
to open their hearts and wallets, so that non-profit
organizations could concentrate on their actual work,
instead of the grinding search for funds.

Independence day Special on Vijay TV 'Desathukku Vanga' (Come to our Nation) Special program on Vijay TV (Tamil narration with English subtitles), covering Payir and Senthil, and the selfless service this US returned young man is providing to the society.

Spirit of India - Youth Special SKG in India Today magazine (please scroll to middle of the page)

"Thenur Sivaji" Payir and SKG in Tamil magazine Kumudam. Tamil version of the article.
Article on Payir and SKG in Tamil Newspaper Dinamalar.

Article on Payir and SKG in The Times Of India Newspaper. Giving Article about SKG in India Empire magazine.

*

What's commendable about Payir is the scale of its ambition. It understands that without a holistic approach to progress, all economic growth exists in a vacuum. It aims to work in rural India to create an atmosphere where people have the space to practice truth. It will lead, create opportunities, facilitate and mentor. It will take a development approach touching all aspects of society — be it local economy and revenue, social needs like health, education, sanitation, infrastructure, civic and panchayat systems. Naturally these processes will help lift the spirit. In an interview with INDIA EMPIRE, founder S.K.G explains how he conceived the project and its future   **- India Empire (2010)**

S.K.G was a mechanical engineer drawing a huge salary in Detroit, US. But four years ago, he decided that it was time to serve the rural poor in his home state. Thanks to that spark in his mind, villagers of Thenur in Perambalur district have an eight bed hospital, a school, a computer center and, above all, an inspiring person to look up to during distress.

"The decision to leave the US was made even before I went there in 1999," says the 35-year-old man. "In fact, the idea to serve the rural poor was born when I was studying in my 11th standard," he added. Even while working in the US, he used to make use of his holidays to visit villages across Tamil Nadu to study their status, their requirements and the extent to which they had been fulfilled by the government. **Times of India (2010)-**

About the author

Jay Kay was born in India; he is prolific writer of poetry in the regional circuit, and a spiritual seeker, an IT professional working in Bangalore, India. He has completed over 10 publications in various titles of Love, Religion and Nature published by pothi.com

He has won several awards in the literary association of the US Journal for a contemporary work in **'The Immortal Expressions'** and **'The Incredible Messiah';** a frequent blogger in face book.

The author can be reached at writerjaykay@gmail.com

*

Publications by the Author

1. The Expedition of Truth

INSPIRATIONAL with profound reflections on Truth with thought provoking snippets

Genre: Philosophy, Science, and Religion (This book is about author's reflections on 'Vethathirium' with ten affirmations of contemporary ten-commandments of truth)

http://pothi.com/pothi/book/ebook-jay-kay-expedition-truth-0

2. From Sex to Spirituality

INSPIRATIONAL with profound reflections on Sex Energy to Spirituality

Genre: Philosophy, Science, and Religion (This book is based on several interviews and the author's insights on social conditioning, adult behavioral psychology and therapy)

http://pothi.com/pothi/book/ebook-jay-kay-transformation-sex-spirituality

3. The Incredible Messiah

INSPIRATIONAL with profound reflections on a Spiritual Master

Genre: Philosophy, Science, and Religion (This book is about a contemporary mystic, Maharishi Vethathiri and his teachings in a nut-shell)

http://pothi.com/pothi/book/ebook-jay-kay-incredible-messiah

4. The Sixth Sense

INSPIRATIONAL with thought provoking anecdote to FREE YOUR MIND

Genre: Philosophy, Science, and Religion (This book is about the potential that you have to expand the sixth sense, which is the ultimate consciousness and an ultimatum to each of you to live through life and conditioning, and ways to get out of addictions)

http://pothi.com/pothi/book/ebook-jay-kay-sixth-sense

5. **The Power of Thought**

    Genre: Philosophy, Science, and Religion (The Power of Thought describes your thoughts originating from Mind. You do not know what to think, you only know how to think! This is exactly the problem as you realize your time is slipping away in wasted life time of endeavor in to mundane tasks. Let us explore the power of your thought and ways to harnessing it for benefits to realizing yourself!!!) http://pothi.com/pothi/book/ebook-jay-kay-power-thought

6. **For the Welfare of Women**

    INSPIRATIONAL with thought snippets for the Welfare of Women

    Genre: Philosophy, Science, and Religion (This book is an invitation to realize the values of women, and Nature's transformation in the evolution of consciousness) http://pothi.com/pothi/book/ebook-lalitha-jaganath-welfare-women